Bas de Gaa[illegible]rtman
Berma Klein Goldewijk

God and the Goods

Global Economy in a Civilizational Perspective

WCC Publications, Geneva

Cover design: Rob Lucas

ISBN 2-8254-1264-3

Printed in the Netherlands

To the memory of

Denys Munby

(1919-1976)

God
and the
Goods

Table of Contents

1. Introduction

The church carries a large responsibility for man's disorder and it is for that responsibility that the churches must give account.

World Council of Churches
Amsterdam Assembly (1948)

Our world today is faced with a threefold crisis of deepening poverty, environmental destruction and social disintegration. Awareness is growing that the roots of this global predicament lie in the absence of a clear link between global economy and a global civilizational perspective. In precisely this area one would expect significant input from a religious angle. Yet the churches seem regrettably absent from the search for new perspectives for transformation. How are global developments to be evaluated? What challenges do they imply for Christianity today? That, in brief, is the subject of this book.

The churches' consistent concern with the future of humankind in general and with social and economic issues in particular has been manifest in ecumenical social ethics and Catholic social teaching. The latter in particular embodies a sustained attempt to understand how societies function and what principles should guide them. The Catholic Church gradually consolidated its social teaching towards the end of the 19th century, notably in Leo XIII's papal encyclical on the "new matters" of misery, injustice and exploitation created by industrialization: *Rerum Novarum* (1891). In both capitalist industrialization and Marxist-Leninist communism the Catholic Church noted the subordination of human well-being to economic ends; and this became the starting point for a series of social encyclicals reconstructing the priority of the human over the economic, and the spiritual and ethical over the material.[1]

Recognizing the continuously changing demands of the "social question", 20th-century Catholic social teaching has developed a set of principles for reflection, criteria for judgment and orientations for action. A body of Protestant social ethics, though less coherent, came into being in the second half of this century. The conceptual basis for this had already been established by the Oxford conference on Church, Community and State (1937). After the Second Vatican Council encouraged local churches to develop their own responses to different realities, national Catholic bishops' conferences produced documents explicitly addressing their national or continental context. Similarly, the founding of the World Council of Churches (WCC) in 1948 not only resulted in socio-economic advocacy at the global level by the new ecumenical body but also encouraged the member churches to address socio-economic issues in their own national, regional and international contexts.

Even so, in regard to the necessary transformation of *global* capitalism the general social thinking of the churches appears to be remarkably lacking in influence. Certainly, *Rerum Novarum* had a surprising impact on workers' emancipation through Catholic trade unionism. Trade unions have always been seen as a representation of the principle of solidarity and the right of association. Other documents have presented strong pleas for land reform, just wages, fair international trade and control of the arms race. In efforts to reform capitalism at a *national* level Christianity has had significant impact–for example, through *Economic Justice for All* by the US Catholic Bishops' Conference (1986) and *The Common Good* by the Catholic Bishops' Conference of England and Wales (1996). In Malawi change of the political status quo was sparked by the 1992 Lenten letter of the Catholic Bishops' Conference.

There is no doubt that the *global* economy and its local manifestations give rise to great concern among the churches. This has come to the forefront in Pope John Paul II's encyclicals *Laborem Exercens* (1981), *Sollicitudo Rei Socialis* (1987) and *Centesimus Annus* (1991), as well as in various policy statements of the assemblies of the World Council of Churches. Yet there is a general apprehension that the churches' relevance as regards the global economy and global civilization is almost negligible. Individual Christians seem largely if not completely to ignore a Christian orientation to society.

How might this be explained? What lies behind the apparent paralysis of organized Christianity? Could new perspectives be found which would offer more meaningful approaches to a world in economic disorder, linking global economy to global civilizational perspectives? What might Christianity contribute to a peaceful coexistence among various peoples, cultures and religions?

The argument in brief

This study explores the dichotomy between economy and civilization in a global perspective. We shall examine past and current approaches of the churches to economic matters, noting that the social teaching of Christian churches has a wealth of resources to motivate, orient and influence the transformation of global capitalism – the priority of the human over the economic; resistance to economic determinism and the concepts of justice and the common good. In reviewing both Catholic social teaching and the ecumenical critique of capitalism as a system for organizing the economy, we shall see that in some ways different types of Christian response to a world in economic disorder appear to have contributed to reforms in the direction of a "social market economy".

But in the face of the threefold crisis of deepening poverty, environmental destruction and social disintegration, the churches show certain signs of paralysis. However appropriate and relevant, the practical social and economic application of the teaching authority of the churches is limited. In the case of Catholic social teaching one reason for this gap between practice and principle may be the Church's own obvious incapacity to apply its social teaching to its internal organization, and in its approach to moral questions, the tension between disclosing social ethics and constraining sexual ethics.

Contemporary Christian response to our global crisis may find inspiration in horizons that are opened up by various old and new forms of thinking globally. Primary among these is the global endeavour for universal human rights, although this project appears to raise considerable conceptual and institutional obstacles, particularly in efforts to implement economic, social and cultural rights.

Various perspectives will be discussed that may assist in finding new ways to overcome these constraints.

Crucial in this study is our concern with possibilities for a basic code of global human coexistence. This leads us to examine the spiritual roots of global crises. Having recognized the spiritual and moral dimensions of the great problems challenging our world, we face the question of how to uncover the genuine spiritual roots of common global civilization. The search is for an original spiritual and moral substance emerging from the primary experience of humanity. The Spirit works in all peoples, believers and non-believers alike, connecting people instead of dividing them, inspiring them towards coexistence and human interaction.

A genuine spirituality may be considered a basic code for interpreting and realizing the global common good. This notion of the common good, or the public interest, will be taken up as a principal focus for efforts towards renewed Christian impact on processes of civilizational change. It demands that all of us examine our own ways of life in the light of Christian faith and the norms of justice. This is the normative setting in which we decide what to produce, what to consume, how to treat others. Basic justice involves overcoming patterns of exclusion and enhancing participation by everyone. Within this perspective of a commitment to the common good, we shall examine the possibilities of replacing a *common ethic of individual rights* with an *ethic of the common good.*

To this, religious spirituality would seem to have a contribution to make. A major challenge lies in transformation from world religions to genuinely global religions. Strategic opportunities present themselves in different types of local response to the global common good. Churches may learn from and join forces with other institutions and people working towards public justice at the global level. To get a clearer view of the possibilities for Christianity to respond adequately to a world in economic disorder, we shall examine the implications of several biblical ideas and themes. Precisely in the area of a global civilizational change from "living for the goods" to recognition of duty, Christianity with its long tradition of critical social thinking and action may have much to contribute.

NOTE

[1] Many of the major social encyclicals were published to mark an anniversary of *Rerum Novarum: Quadragesimo Anno* in 1931 (Pius XI), *Mater et Magistra* in 1961 (John XXIII), *Octogesimo Adveniens* in 1971 (Paul VI), *Laborem Exercens* in 1981 and *Centesimus Annus* in 1991 (John Paul II). Other relevant encyclicals include *Pacem in Terris* (1963, John XXIII), *Populorum Progressio* (1967, Paul VI) and *Sollicitudo Rei Socialis* (1987, John Paul II). In addition, mention should be made of the Pastoral Constitution of the Second Vatican Council on the Church in the Modern World (*Gaudium et Spes*, 1965).

2. The Dialectics of Global Economy and Global Civilization

I see a large, yet typical, paradox for our era in the fact that, though contemporary humanity has been aware of these dangers, it does almost nothing to confront or avert them.

Vaclav Havel, 1997

Globalization is a predominant pattern in contemporary social change. It involves the manifestation of forces which shape the lives of people at a global rather than a territorially linked level (the local or national). Indeed, Robertson describes it as a process transforming the world into *one single place*.[1] Its facets include trade and finance, corporate activity, standard-setting (common scales of measurement as well as universal human rights), culture (including global consumerism), ecology (for example, effects on the global climate and the ozone layer) and a growing *consciousness* of the world as one single place.[2]

Globalization, according to Peter Beyer, displays both continuity and discontinuity with modernization.[3] It replaces modernization in the sense of expanding vital institutions of Western modernization to the rest of the globe: the capitalist economy, the nation-state, scientific rationality and communication technology. This element of "imperialistic" expansion is a constant theme in the globalization discussion. Once it is seen as an exogenous process in all parts of the globe except for the West, globalization becomes identical to Western imperialism. And indeed it would not have happened had it not first occurred in the West.[4]

Yet globalization is more than the expansion of a Western culture at the expense of other cultures. Something novel has emerged: the creation of a *new global culture* which is becoming the wider social context of all particular contexts, including those of the West. Like all other particular cultures, Western cultures are also relativized and intrinsically changed in the process of globalization.[5] Therefore, the extension of global social reality is as much at the expense of Western culture as of any other. Does globalization then mean a progressive homogenization of all cultures, so that in the future only global culture will exist? Or does it imply a transformation, a change of contexts, but not the disappearance of particular identities?

People's efforts to preserve, protect or stabilize their particular identities appear to become negated, relativized and often marginalized in processes of global change. But Beyer maintains that while the global system corrodes inherited cultural or personal identities, it also encourages the re-creation or revitalization of particular identities: not just to create meaning but also to gain control over the direction of change, to shape global reality, to construct one's own way of inclusion in the global system.[6] This observation definitely holds in regard to the economy.

Economic and financial globalization

Economic globalization may be seen as "both a rise in economic activity that is worldwide in scope and a growing intensification of economic flows and activities across societies and between people".[7] Thus, it relates to the growing extent of world trade. The majority of countries today trade with the majority of others.[8] But globalization relates as well as to its intensity, with a current world export-world production ratio of about 20 percent. According to the UN Human Development Report of 1994, transnational corporations (TNCs) presently conduct 70 percent of global trade. The growing importance of TNCs is also illustrated by the current figure for *intra*-company trade of 30 percent of the global figure.

Korten speaks of a "second industrial revolution".[9] The first industrial revolution replaced muscle power by machines. Through tariff structures, much of the immediate unemployment created by increasing labour productivity in this way was shifted to the colonies (in the textiles industry, for example). The second industrial revolution is based on the exploitation of information and communication technology. Computers and electronic sensors can "give machines eyes, ears and brains to see and hear, interpret and act". If this development continues, it might lead to corporations with almost no human workers and managers. This would indeed "represent capitalism at its very purest, completely unconcerned with anything but safe profit and power".

This second industrial revolution, Korten argues, is also based on processes of colonization, now "defined more by class than by geography and forcing ever more of the world's population in the ranks of the colonized". This analysis corresponds with predictions of a global development in the direction of a "20:80 society", in which 20 percent of the people participate actively in the economy with ever-increasing work burdens, while the remaining 80 percent have to satisfy themselves with hardly any work in the formal sector of the economy and a meagre income. In the United States increased working hours and burdens have already been documented. For those who are excluded, a modern form of "bread and circuses" – on the screen – will be available.

In the same vein, we may speak of a first and second *financial* revolution. The first, in the second half of the 19th century, manifested itself particularly in the growing importance of financial titles or securities. Previously wealth had been incorporated in real estate and hence displayed a certain degree of visibility and accessibility – depending on the relative success of processes of socialization of private property. Now it became hidden and embodied in movable holdings. More than 50 years ago Georges Ripert already spoke of the "revolutionary increase" in movable wealth in France: from a total capital of 9 billion francs in 1850 to 115 billion in 1912, a 1200 percent rise in 62 years.[10] The second financial revolution has been from real trade in actual currencies and securities to electronic claims regarding future values. Financial globalization is primarily evident in the increase of foreign exchange trading: from around US$15 billion in 1973 to about US$60 billion in 1983 to some US$1200 billion in 1997. The trade in financial titles is now primarily in "derivatives" (options, swaps, futures), a business in which fortunes may be accumulated in no time. The Eurodollar market has reached an amount of over US$4000 billion. The total financial turnover exceeds world trade in real values by a factor of 50.

Such developments naturally affect the nature of capitalism. Illustrative of what Lash and Urry called *The End of Organized Capitalism* (in their 1987 book) is what happened to Barings Bank in 1995. In a world of *hedging*, *arbitration*, *futures* (including *forwards*) and *margin calls*, a world in which more than US$1000 billion daily circulates in security derivatives alone and one individual can "move markets", corporate risk appears to be acceptable even though bankruptcy may involve banks of high repute. *System risk* is still another matter, as the salvaging operation for Mexico in early 1995 demonstrated. But few would deny that in this blitz world a collapse of the whole global financial system is a serious risk.[11]

Korten uses the example of Mexico to illustrate the high price the world has to pay for economic and financial globalization. In 1993-1994 a populist government attracted an enormous amount of foreign capital. A mere 10 percent of this ended up in the real sphere. The rest fell into the hands of people who apparently had the power to use it for purely financial investments; and in that brief period ten Mexican nationals joined the ranks of US-dollar billionaires. In December 1994 the peso collapsed. For a short while the central bank supported the national currency, thus transferring its dollar reserves to those who speculated against the peso. After the inevitable devaluation, a programme of budget cuts had to be carried out which cost 750,000 people their jobs.

Global capitalism as described here is truly post-modern, in the sense that it is detached from the earlier norms which guided capitalist reform after the first industrial revolution. Its manifestations are described by Lash and Urry as rapidly moving capital flows, fewer collective contracts, reduced power of both trade unions and central government, easy shifting of manufacturing activities to new regions and smaller sizes of each establishment. "Blitz capital" aims at quick short-term profits rather than moderate long-term profitability. Indeed, the world is moving towards a *24-hour economy* in which employment is no longer a major managerial concern. In post-modern capitalism anything goes – anywhere, anytime, anyhow.

Multiple global crises

This global economy lacks strong political institutions. The "New International Economic Order" which was the subject of two special sessions of the United Nations in the 1970s did not materialize. Real commodity prices in the 1990s were 45 percent lower than in the 1980s. As a result, the terms of trade for the developing countries have been reduced by half over the past 25 years.[12] Global losses through trade protection, immigration barriers and increasing debt burdens amount to ten times the aid developing countries receive. In fact, the *interest* on its current debt which the Third World pays to the industrialized nations is more than twice what it receives in official development aid. Despite its growing impoverishment, Africa is still faced with a net outflow of financial resources. During the past two decades the least developed countries have seen their share of world trade reduced from 0.6 percent to 0.3 percent; in fact, foreign direct investment bypasses more than half of all developing countries.[13] Clearly, globalization has its downside – *exclusion*, with the ensuing processes of social disintegration. We shall now briefly review some of its effects.

Deepening poverty. Capitalism has always been plagued by socio-economic inequality and the lack of protection against poverty and destitution. The UN Human Development Report in 1992 estimated the ratio of income distribution in the world between the one billion people at the top and the one billion at the bottom at 150:1. Although the proportion of poor people in the world as a whole appears to have fallen considerably, in absolute terms the situation is frightfully disturbing: an estimated 1.3 billion people – more than one-fourth of the world's population – have to survive on the equivalent of less than one US dollar per day.[14] The average annual income for an inhabitant of the globe today is almost US$5000, a figure which makes the severe poverty of hundreds of millions of human beings "a scandal – reflecting shameful inequalities and inexcusable failures of national and international policy".[15]

It should be noted that enrichment and exclusion are not two distinct and separate processes. As Charles Elliott has argued, "both exclusion and downward mobility, which are no more than the processes of relative and absolute impoverishment, are most frequently the reverse image of the enrichment of another group".[16] This has become most evident at the global level. As far as global structures of production, finance and trade are concerned, the words of the ancient Greek historian Thucydides still apply: "The strong do what is in their power and the weak accept their fate."

Intra-state collective violence. A great concern in the world today is the growth of intra-state collective violence. While the horrifying atrocities of wars such as those in Sudan, Liberia, Somalia, Rwanda, Sri Lanka and Afghanistan may be incomprehensible and inexplicable, it is undeniable that socio-economic deprivation breeds violence. In the case of "ordinary" crime, this link is well-known. As Kaplan says, "where there has always been mass poverty, people find liberation in violence".[17] Similarly, even a quick look at the ranking of countries in the UN's Human Development Index (HDI) over the 1990s reveals that armed conflicts have been located primarily in countries at the bottom of the list and have been almost absent in the so-called First World. Here again the world today manifests its dual character.

Jobless growth. An essential objective of any national economic policy is the promotion of full employment. But a striking contemporary phenomenon is "jobless growth", depicted and illustrated in the UN's 1993 Human Development Report. Between 1980 and 1993 the world's 500 largest corporations dropped 4.4 million jobs, while increasing their sales by a factor of 1.4, their assets by a factor of 2.3 and compensation for their corporate executive officers by a factor of 6.1.[18] In both the industrialized and the industrializing worlds, long-term unemployment is growing at highly disturbing rates. In Western Europe one in ten workers is unemployed, and 40 percent of them have been without a job for more than a year. In Eastern Europe one in seven has no paid employment. For Africa, Asia, South and Central America the figures are much higher. The International Labour Office (ILO) suggests in its *World Employment Report 1995* that this is not so much the result of globalization and technological change as a lack of choices in the fields of economic policy and economic order. While labour productivity will continue to rise, the rise of total production cannot keep pace, if only for ecological reasons. With current labour-saving techniques we can only expect a further increase of global unemployment.

Environmental destruction. An environmental crisis has become noticeable at three different levels of community: *globally*, as manifested in climate change and threats to the ozone layer; *regionally*, as manifested in acid rain (Europe), deforestation, loss of biodiversity (South America and Asia), land degradation and desertification (Africa); and *locally*, as manifested in soil and water pollution, and various indications of absolute resource scarcity. Without a strong international system of states, any hope of tackling these crises effectively is bound to remain an illusion.

Global civilization in jeopardy

Humanity has evolved in different civilizations which have gradually and in diverse ways shaped people's habits, relationships to the world, models of behaviour and values. There is a growing awareness today that humankind finds itself at a crossroads. As the old polarities of left and right appear increasingly outdated, unprecedented possibilities for reshaping social relationships and institutions are emerging. Grasping these prospects requires a thorough understanding of the interconnectedness of global economy and global civilization and a recognition of the dehumanizing tendencies in global society.

After the major political upheavals of this century – two world wars, the collapse of colonialism and the fall of real existing socialism – no new mode of global coexistence among peoples, cultures and religions has yet emerged. In a time of rapid globalization this poses a significant problem. In this context the work of Samuel Huntington has attracted a great deal of attention.[19]

Huntington believes that the confrontation between ideologies of the 20th century is giving way in the post-cold war era to a confrontation between civilizations. Moreover, the identities of people have been shifting from state and ideology to civilization. Huntington defines a civilization as the highest cultural grouping of people and the broadest level of cultural identity people possess, that which distinguishes humans from other species. His central thesis is that while the world as a whole is increasingly accepting the new habits of global civilization, ancient traditions are reviving. As different religions and cultures awake to new ways of being, they are seeking new room to exist precisely around that which makes them different from others. Conflict in the post cold-war world will thus be sparked by civilizational confrontations in which the primary identification of people will no longer be ideological – rooted in fascism, socialism or democracy – but cultural.

Huntington identifies six major existing civilizations: Western civilization built on Catholicism and Protestantism (Western Europe and North America), the civilization built on the Orthodox Church (Russia and Eastern Europe), Islamic civilization, Hindu civilization, Chinese civilization and Japanese civilization. South America and Sub-Saharan Africa have the potential to become distinct civilizations of their own but in Huntington's view they do not as yet possess the conditions necessary to qualify as major civilizations. In five of Huntington's six civilizations clear "core states" can be discerned: the Western (the European Union and North America), the Orthodox (Russia), the Hindu (India), the Chinese (China) and the Japanese civilization (Japan). Huntington believes that there is no such core state in the Islamic civilization.

In this global context, Western civilization is thus just one of the major civilizations. Since strong and mature civilizations tend to reject the influence of others, it is not to be expected that Western civilization will become a universal one; Huntington believes that the effort of Western countries to propagate their civilization to the rest of the world is fruitless and dangerous. Instead they should join forces to defend themselves against the challenges posed by other civilizations. Faced with conflicts arising within different civilizational spheres, the best thing for the West to do would be to leave everything to the control and management by its "core state", the European Union and the United States.

Huntington regards the Islamic and Chinese civilizations as posing the greatest potential threats to Western civilization. The former could become a major threat if conflicts within this civilization continue to deepen without a core state playing the role of effective mediator. The latter will constitute a menace to the West if China as a state becomes too powerful. Huntington refers not only to struggles *between* but also *within* civilizations. Such confrontations, he argues, will dominate and reconfigure global politics.

The initial reactions to Huntington's thesis – including in the United States and Western Europe – have been largely critical. It has been observed that while he draws attention to the growing impact of cultural differences in a globalizing world, he seems not to recognize that different civilizations not only clash with each other but that their confrontation can also lead to exchange and transformation. Others have noted that he makes no clear distinction between civilization and culture, that civilizations are not in fact as cohesive as he depicts them, that he has no elaborated view of multiculturalism, and that his portrayals of non-Western cultures and civilizations may be seriously disputed.

Without entering more deeply into the debate about Huntington's work we must nevertheless acknowledge one crucial fact: global humanity today is not so much driven by ideology as by religion and culture – that is, by identities. Furthermore, "*civilization*" does indeed seem to be the paradigm in which actors like the nation state and political forces are operating. What is lacking in Huntington's analysis of possible clashes of civilizations is an examination of *global* civilizational perspectives – to which we shall turn later in this present study.

Our enquiry is set in this context of a world in economic disorder and of global civilization in jeopardy. Acknowledging that spirituality and ethical orientations have always been regarded as the "core business" of the churches, we shall ask how the churches position themselves today in regard to the global socio-economic and political context on the one hand and the renewed search for value-orientation and global civilization on the other. Clearly, this is not the first time the churches have been challenged to respond to processes of change of a civilizational nature. Three different approaches may be discerned – secular redemption, fundamental rejection and critical valuation – and it is around these three approaches that the overview of Christian concerns with economic matters to which we now turn is structured.

NOTES

[1] R. Robertson, *Globalization: Social Theory and Global Culture*, London, Newbury Park, California, and New Delhi, Sage Publications, 1992.

[2] Cf. J.A. Scholte, "Globalization and Social Change", The Hague, Institute of Social Studies, State and Society Relations Paper no. 97-3, 1997, p.222.

[3] P.F. Beyer, *Religion and Globalization*, London, Sage Publications, 1994, p.8.

[4] *Ibid.*

[5] *Ibid.*, p.9.

[6] *Ibid.*, p.3.

[7] J. Perraton, D. Goldblatt, D. Held and A. McGrew, "The Globalization of Economic Activity", *New Political Economy*, Vol. 2, no. 2, July 1997.

[8] Cf. T. Nierop, *Systems and Regions in Global Politics*, Chicago, John Wiley, 1994, ch.3.

[9] D. Korten, *When Corporations Rule the World*, San Francisco, Barrett-Koehler, 1995, p.240.

[10] Cf. Georges Ripert, *Aspects juridiques du capitalisme moderne*, Paris, Librairie Générale de Droit et de Jurisprudence, 1946.

[11] On the Barings Bank collapse, see *The Economist*, 4-10 March 1995. If it had been Chase Manhattan Bank rather than Barings which had gone bankrupt, the collapse of the global financial situation would have been close. Some have noted that major earthquakes in Tokyo or California might also spark system collapse by resulting in a sudden and tremendous reduction of the value of real assets. For an analysis of the Mexican case, see F. Chesnay, "Une crise financière de type nouveau au Mexique: défense et illustration de la dictature des marchés", *Le Monde diplomatique*, March 1995, pp.28f.

[12] UN Development Programme, *Human Development Report 1997*, p.9.

[13] *Ibid.*

[14] *Ibid.*, p.5.

[15] *Ibid.*, p.2.

16 C. M. Elliott, *Patterns of Poverty in the Third World*, New York, Praeger, 1975.

17 R. D. Kaplan, "The Coming Anarchy", *Atlantic Monthly*, Feb. 1994, p.72.

18 Rob van Drimmelen, "Globalization" (unpublished paper, WCC, Geneva, 1996), p.4.

19 S. Huntington's thesis was first developed in his article "The Clash of Civilizations", *Foreign Affairs*, Vol. 72, no.3, summer 1993, pp.2-26. This formed the basis of his subsequent book *The Clash of Civilizations and the Remaking of World Order*, New York, Simon & Schuster, 1996. Cf. also S. Sato, "Clash of Civilizations or Self-Renovation through Mutual Learning: On Huntington's Treatise 'Clash of Civilizations' ", Institute for International Policy Studies and Okamoto International Affairs Research Institute, July 1997.

3. Christian Response to a World in Economic Disorder

To separate the spiritual aspects of Hebrew-Christian religion from the economic is impossible, for all life is one piece.
V. Obenhaus (1965)

Christianity may be seen as the most materially oriented of all world religions. Indeed, welfare and happiness are regarded as not so much a vice as a virtue or, at least, a legitimate concern. Several biblical images reflect this concern – from the portrayal of life in the Garden of Eden as good in every respect, including its material aspects, to Israel's exodus from oppression in Egypt, which would lead to a land of milk and honey, to the final destination of humankind, the New Jerusalem, which is described as a luxurious city with foundations of jewels, streets of gold and gates of pearl (Rev. 21:21). This is of course a vision, but it is noteworthy that heaven and earth are not so separated that they do not relate to each other. Indeed, the realm of God includes the world of the goods.

Secular redemption

From this perspective, Christian concern with economic matters is, understandably, primarily constructive, in the sense of taking a positive attitude towards material welfare. Indeed, Elliott even speaks of "secular redemption":

> Economic growth is... a means to what we may call secular redemption: the eradication of the environmental factors that limit and falsify and corrupt the human spirit. Disease, ignorance, superstition, boredom and monotony – these are the cancers of the human spirit that economic and social development should strive to eradicate.[1]

Hence it is not surprising that Christianity has been interpreted as a cultural factor spurring the development of capitalist society. As is well-known, Max Weber connected the Protestant ethic particularly with Calvinism which, like Lutheranism, stressed the idea of vocation but also connected this to daily work in a transcendental perspective. "For the Calvinist the rectification of the evils of the world itself became an integral part of the fulfilment of his calling."[2] Thus, the acquisition of goods could later be seen as a symbol of God's favourable attitude towards a zealous worker.[3]

Van Leeuwen even argued that it was Christianity as such which brought about modernization in its Western sense: "[The] technological revolution was nurtured in the bosom of Christian civilization and indeed is one of its children."[4] Strikingly, this modern interpretation of progress has led others to make a fundamentally *negative* Christian response to the existing economic order.

Fundamental rejection

When Nassau Senior, the first professor of political economy at Oxford, asserted in his inaugural lecture that the pursuit of wealth is "the great source of *moral* improvement" to the mass of humanity, Cardinal Newman reacted violently: "One is taken by surprise on meeting with so categorical a contradiction of our Lord, St Paul, St Chrysostom, St Leo, and all saints."[5] Surprising or not, Nassau Senior's view is still very much alive. Typical is the moral justification of capitalism offered by an editorialist in *The Economist* in January 1994:

> Capitalism is a species of freedom. Give people certain rights (such as the rights to own property and sell their labour) then leave them alone and capitalism is what you get. Capitalism is a good thing mainly because freedom is a good thing.

In effect, this version of the ideology of capitalism identifies the system with freedom in the negative sense of being left alone.

The Dutch economist Bob Goudzwaard describes the Western belief in progress as a genuine *faith*, a faith with the power to move mountains. It is a "consistent and goal-oriented system for the promotion of economic and technological progress". Goudzwaard sees this as a rather "closed" obsession, quoting Löwith's article on "The Fate of Progress":

An uncanny coincidence of fatalism and a will to progress presently characterizes all contemporary thinking about the future course of history. Progress now threatens us; it has become our fate... [We are] *set free* and yet *imprisoned* by our own power... Progress itself goes on progressing; we can no longer stop it or turn it around.

This analysis leads to a plea for a *disclosure* of society, requiring among other things an end to utilitarianism and a reversal of our "happiness horizon" from quantitative interpretations of progress to meaningful labour.[6]

Goudzwaard's argument falls in the tradition of denouncing what is considered to be an un-Christian economic order and prophetically proclaiming the need for conversion. The problem is materialism and modernity as such. As Emil Brunner put it in a background document for the founding assembly of the World Council of Churches in Amsterdam in 1948: "The modern world has lost the horizon of transcendence. This is the basic fact of the social disorder."[7]

Crucial in such reflections is the relationship between God and the goods. Actually, a highly restrictive attitude towards individualist materialism goes back to the early church. In the middle ages attempts were made to separate Christian life-styles from the prevailing economic order. At the same time, the church established clear constraints on individualistic materialism and the lust for money through doctrines such as *justum pretium* – the requirement of fair prices and wages – and the prohibition of usury. Asceticism still finds expression in the life of certain sects that aim at direct personal fellowship between their members.

Today, negative Christian responses to the economy focus especially on the international economic (dis)order. For example, the concluding statement of a meeting organized by the WCC in São Paulo in 1987, entitled "Churches, Christians and Economic Systems: A Call for Obedient Discipleship", invites congregations, churches and Christian groups "to join in resisting the evil manifestation of the prevailing economic system as a fundamental matter of Christian faith and confession".[8] "Resisting capitalism" is seen as a direct consequence of "confessing Christ". Like apartheid and the use of nuclear weapons, the prevailing international economic order is thus seen as a *status confessionis*–a condition in which taking a confessional stand is not optional but necessary.[9] The São Paulo appeal is itself in the line of such earlier declarations of the WCC as the statement by its assembly in Nairobi in 1975: "While we confess a Christ who frees and unites, the economic structures in which we live tend to enslave to wealth and divide."

In this connection one can also refer to papal encyclicals such as *Sollicitudo Rei Socialis*, in which Pope John Paul II speaks of structures of sin:

> The sum total of the negative factors working against a true awareness of the universal common good, and the need to further it, gives the impression of creating, in persons and institutions, an obstacle which is difficult to overcome. If the present situation can be attributed to difficulties of various kinds, it is not out of place to speak of "structures of sin", which... are rooted in personal sin, and thus always linked to the concrete acts of individuals who introduce these structures, consolidate them and make them difficult to remove. And thus they grow stronger, spread and become the source of other sins, and so influence people's behaviour (para. 36).

Sollicitudo Rei Socialis builds on the final document of the conference of Latin American bishops in Puebla (1979), in which institutionalized injustice was theologically qualified as a social sin (cf. paras 29, 328, 1269, 1305). Yet, it is not enough simply to condemn and reject such structures. The challenge is to find other ways of structuring society so that people may realize their dignity and achieve their rights. As the Catholic bishops of the Netherlands put it in their Lenten letter of 1973:

> But structures are not things that stand apart from us, which we could change without changing ourselves. It is our ends, our views, our norms, in short our mentality, which are incorporated in these social structures. In their turn these structures influence our mentality and attitude, too (paras 14-15).

Critical valuation

The prevalent attitude towards contemporary socio-economic structures in both the Roman Catholic Church and the World Council of Churches may be characterized as one of "critical valuation". Criteria for this have been gradually established in a rather coherent body of Catholic social teaching, but before summarizing these principles it may be helpful to situate them in the development of Catholic social teaching as a whole.

The shaping of the social teaching of the Catholic Church has been a continuous undertaking which has manifested remarkable developments, involving changes in the social magisterium which have in turn often provoked ideological controversy and debate. The focus of concern has gradually extended from Western Europe to the whole globe. Whereas earlier social encyclicals concentrated on a natural law basis, more recent documents drew on a broader search for truth in all human sciences.

While there are many interpretations of Catholic social teaching and its evolution, many specialists would identify three different stages with three distinct focal points. Some would describe this as a development from "corporatism" to "reformism" to "radicalism"; others would speak of the transition from traditional to progressive liberal to radical, though without linear evolution and sometimes co-existing.

Corporatism based on association (which is not to be equated with the state corporatism of Italy under Mussolini or Portugal under Salazar) was characterized by the project of reconstructing a "new Christendom". This tendency began in the 1930s with the encyclical *Quadragesimo Anno* (1931) and continued until the second world war. After the war social teaching aligned itself with the democratic and reformist approaches represented by Christian Democratic parties in Europe but remained open to new analyses of economic progress and development often linked to earlier types of social Christian thinking. In the 1960s, especially after the Second Vatican Council, social doctrine came under growing criticism as an abstract and atemporal ideology, linked to mere reformism, insufficiently operative and too connected with a European perspective. In response, interpreters agree, something new emerged in the social magisterium in the 1960s, though they diverge on the precise location of this change, which manifested itself over time and in subsequent pontificates.[10]

In the 1980s, with the encyclical *Laborem Excercens*, a further step was taken, signalled by its insistence "that the social question must be dealt with in its whole complex dimension" (para. 7). The form and method of dealing with the social question changed. The approach to reality from a fixed conceptual framework gave way to a reading of reality inductively while discerning its signs in the light of the gospel. Chenu locates this change already in *Octogesima Adveniens* (1971).[11]

A rather different interpretation is offered by Michael Novak, who incorporates social teaching into a framework of liberal economic individualism:

> As Leo XIII won the name "pope of associations" for himself because he made free associations central to his social teaching, so 100 years from now John Paul II may be accorded fame as "the pope of economic enterprise", because he made "personal economic initiative" central to his social teaching.

It is certainly true that Catholic social teaching recognizes the positive values of the market, private property, business and free human creativity in the economic sector. It also sets forth democratic concepts of human rights and religious freedom in regard to state intervention. *Sollicitudo Rei Socialis* does not manifest the tendency to blame the West for everything which has been detected in Pope Paul VI's encyclical *Populorum Progressio* (1967). But to proclaim John Paul II the champion of economic enterprise misinterprets his contribution to social teaching. In his assessment of *Sollicitudo Rei Socialis*, John Kenneth Galbraith comes to an evaluation significantly different from Novak's:

> The encyclical letter takes issue squarely with one of the more entrenched positions of our time, one that also has powerful theological overtones. That is the belief of many well-endowed people, including, one imagines, a certain number of conservative Catholics, that government, in the words of President Reagan, is not the remedy but the problem in any approach to the poor. Its role should be restricted severely; the burden of proof must always be on public action; only national defense, military expenditure, is sacrosanct... Here is an uncompromising collision of faiths, and in this confronta-

tion there can be no doubt where the pope stands – the encyclical makes this wholly clear.[12]

The Catholic Church has always been concerned with socio-economic conditions. It has clear views on these; and while it is still updating its interpretation of them (for example, on such issues as fair wages, land reform, gender and environmental challenges), there is an undoubted continuity in Catholic social teaching. Coherent with its principles, social teaching is a plea for the basic humanity that is to be found in every human being. Another element of continuity, contrary to Novak, is that the Catholic Church does not regard all projects for the organization of society as equally valid. Gustavo Gutiérrez, whose point of departure differs from Galbraith's, explicitly honours Pope John Paul II because of his re-examination, from the perspective of the preferential option for the poor, of *Rerum Novarum.*[13] Indeed, in *Centesimus Annus* John Paul II describes *Rerum Novarum* as

> an excellent testimony to the continuity within the Church of the so-called "preferential option for the poor", an option which I defined as a "special form of primacy in the exercise of Christian charity" [*SRS* 42]. Pope Leo's encyclical on the "condition of the workers" is thus an encyclical on the poor and on the terrible conditions to which the new and often violent process of industrialization had reduced great multitudes of people (para. 11).

The development in Catholic social teaching can perhaps best be illustrated in regard to one of the continuous themes of the social *magisterium*: the inevitability of conflict. At the end of the last century, Leo XIII was faced with a new concept of state and authority, and a new way of dealing with property and labour. Labour forces appeared to be treated as factors of production, regulated by a law of supply and demand, thus dividing society, provoking conflict and leading to injustice and inhumane conditions. In response, *Rerum Novarum* affirmed that the Catholic Church does not condemn social conflict as such. *Quadragesimo Anno*, *Laborem Exercens* and *Centesimus Annus* all reaffirm the positive side of social conflict, so long as there is abstention from violence and reciprocal hatred and to the extent that it is a component of the struggle for human dignity and social justice.[14] John Paul II even declares that conflicts in the socio-economic sector are inevitable (*Centesimus Annus*, para. 5). Faced with these conflicts the Church does not react with models, but with ethical and human demands.

Principles of Catholic social teaching

The social magisterium has elaborated distinct principles of Catholic social teaching. While subject to different interpretations,[15] these may be summarized as follows:

1. *Human dignity:* human beings are created in the image and likeness of God, and they do not lose this because of poverty or other setbacks. People are more important than goods, "to be" supersedes "to have".

2. *Community and the common good:* the human person also reflects the image of God in constituting a *social* being. Dignity and rights are realized in community, in relationship with others. The common good represents all those conditions of social life – economic, political, cultural – which make it possible for persons to achieve dignity and humanity.

3. *Rights and responsibilities:* people have a fundamental right to life, food, shelter, health care, education and employment. Individual rights, however, always manifest themselves within the context of the common good. People have a fundamental right to participate in decisions that affect their lives; they have a responsibility to respect the rights of others and a duty to work for the common good. These rights and responsibilities are to be protected by all institutions in society.

4. *The option for the poor:* the claims of the poor have a preferential status because their needs are the most urgent. Thus all public policy decisions must be evaluated in terms of how they affect the poor.

5. *Economic justice and solidarity:* people do not exist for the economy but the economy for the people. Hence the resources of the earth are to be shared. Labour takes precedence over capital and technology. Just wages and the right to organize are to be respected and protected.

6. *Subsidiarity:* responsibilities should be placed and decisions

should be taken as close as possible to the level of individual initiative in local communities and institutions. Centralized government structures are necessary when social coordination and regulation at a higher level are indispensable to the realization of the common good.

7. *Promotion of peace:* peace, as a fruit of justice, depends on the right order among people and among nations. To promote peace and establish the right conditions for it, effective international authority is essential.

On the basis of such principles the existing order is regularly assessed. Regarding the economy the prevailing attitude has generally been critical. Of course there have to be processes of production, distribution and consumption of goods and services, but the church is especially concerned with the effect of these on human dignity and social justice.

As the world conference on Church, Community and State (Oxford 1937) put it:

> Man cannot live without bread, and man cannot live by bread alone... In the economic sphere the first duty of the church is to insist that economic activities, like every other department of human life, stand under the judgment of Christ.[16]

The critique of capitalism. As a manifestation of people's lives in relation to nature and in community with their fellow human beings, the economy falls under normative biblical notions such as stewardship – the earth belongs to God – and love. This has led to critical observations regarding four characteristics of the capitalist economic order outlined by the Oxford conference: the enhancement of acquisitiveness, inequalities, irresponsible possession of economic power and the frustration of the sense of Christian vocation.

The enhancement of acquisitiveness. Capitalism is based on Adam Smith's concept of a "natural progress of opulence".[17] Indeed, "we find no concept of progress before the advent of capitalism".[18] This progress comes primarily through specialization in production and division of labour. It is *natural* in the sense that people should be left free to follow their natural inclinations: "the drive to get ahead, to make money, to accumulate capital".[19] The result is an "acquisitive society" in which values have generally become money values. Tawney described its essence as follows:

> [It] makes the individual the centre of his own universe, and dissolves moral principles into a choice of expediencies. And it immensely simplifies the problems of social life in complex communities. For it relieves them of the necessity of discriminating between different types of economic activity and different sources of wealth, between enterprise and avarice, energy and unscrupulous greed, property which is legitimate and property which is theft, the just enjoyment of the fruits of labour and the idle parasitism of birth or fortune, because it treats all economic activities at the same level.[20]

Wicksteed has argued that the economic motive is not so much egoism as "non-tuism" – in the sense that the economic relation "does not exclude from my mind everyone but me; it potentially includes everyone but you".[21] Even St Paul produced his tents not to please his clients but to earn a living. Indeed, there is no realistic way back to subsistence economies. Modern economies are based on specialization in production and exchange. In such a setting Christians too must accept that an *effective* organization of economic life – in the sense of having an adequate capacity to provide the food, clothing, shelter and other goods which the community requires – cannot easily be founded on a different motive. Since the fall of the Berlin wall and the proven *political* impossibility of real existing socialism, this has become a global understanding.[22]

Yet two major questions remain. The first is whether contemporary capitalism really is in all respects a system for the production of goods people *need*. Second, does capitalism create the right conditions for human integrity in all its different aspects? The church will continue to be concerned with the *absolutization* of the pursuit of wealth. There is no pure economics, since other aspects of human behaviour play their part, too; and economics is not inherently ethics. Thus, the challenge to keep economics connected to morality always remains.

Inequalities. Theoretically, socio-economic inequalities in a capitalist economic order should be of merely minor significance, because competition would result in processes of continuous elimination of profits. In practice, however, the ways in which industrialized society distributes wealth result in extreme inequalities and deprivation for the majority of people. What Oxford noted in 1937 had been observed six year earlier in Pius XI's encyclical *Quadragesimo Anno*, published forty years after *Rerum Novarum*:

> Just freedom of action must, of course, be left both to individual citizens and to families, yet only on condition that the common good be preserved and wrong to any individual be abolished. The function of the rulers of the state, moreover, is to watch over the community and its parts; but in protecting private individuals in their rights, chief consideration ought to be given to the weak and the poor (para. 25).

Oxford linked the issue of socio-economic rights to Christian duty: "Christians cannot be in doubt as to the primary duty of ensuring that the conditions required for full personal development are enjoyed by the whole of the rising generation." Furthermore it noted the role of discrimination on the basis of cultural identity factors: "disadvantages are greatly increased where economic opportunities are denied on racial grounds".

Half a century later, the accent in addressing the issue of inequality and deprivation has shifted to the international setting. A case in point is the sharp condemnation of economic (dis)order in a report from the WCC's sixth assembly (Vancouver 1983). The statement calls on the churches to respond in ways that go beyond mere prophetic denunciation:

> The machine of the prevailing economic order starves millions of people, and increases the number of unemployed every year... We interpret this development as idolatry, stemming from human sin, a product of satanic forces. We are in a situation where we must go beyond the normal prophetic and intercessory action of the churches... The church is thus challenged not only in what it does, but in its very faith and being.[23]

This formulation foreshadows the *status confessionis* posed by the "Call" from São Paulo in 1987, cited earlier, which concludes:

> The prevailing economic systems are in their foundations contrary to the intentions of God's creation, resulting in poverty, injustice, powerlessness and death..., [while] the structures of the powerful,

> mainline Western churches are aligned with, reflect, defend, benefit from, and are also imprisoned by these systems of death.

Whether or not Christians today would endorse this rather radical call to obedient discipleship, the challenge remains to work towards an international economic order that provides "for the basic needs, human rights, democratic empowerment and life for people". A Catholic expression of this same concern for economic justice appears in Pope Paul VI's document "Justice in the World" (1971):

> Both within the national communities and at the international plane there should be more justice in the distribution of goods. In regard to world trade the power relations should be superseded by agreements aiming at the common good... One should have the courage to revise the current system of international relations in regard to international distribution of production, trade structures, profit control, monetary policy... In this way the growth models of the rich countries will be put into question... Many people now go as far as questioning the very model of our society itself.

Irresponsible possession of economic power. The preoccupation voiced by Oxford over the concentration of economic power is already found in *Rerum Novarum*:

> The present age handed over the workers... to the inhumanity of employers and the unbridled greed of competitors. A devouring usury, although often condemned by the Church, but practised nevertheless under another form by avaricious and grasping men, has increased the evil; and in addition the whole process of production as well as trade in every kind of goods has been brought almost entirely under the power of a few, so that a very few rich and exceedingly rich men have laid a yoke almost of slavery on the unnumbered masses of non-owning workers (para. 6).

The organizing principle of capitalism is free exchange–the market–based on the legal foundations of property and contract.[24] It is the principle of *private property* which connects economic decisions and incentives. This connection is held to be essential. Where the risk lies, there the control should be: "The power of making decisions will be most wisely exercised if it rests in the hands of those who stand to lose most heavily if the decision turns out badly."[25]

From a Christian perspective two issues are particularly noteworthy here.

The first is that Christianity cannot condone absolute notions of property. Property is relative, while always having a social function, since all human beings have a right to share in God's gifts. Already in the fourth century, Bishop Ambrose of Milan (339-397) argued that giving to the poor is restitution of stolen goods: "You are not making a gift of your possessions to the poor person. You are handing over to him what is his."[26] Ambrose is not here rejecting the right of private property but the violation of the property rights of the poor. John Chrysostom confirms the same perspective:

> The rich are in the possession of the goods of the poor, even if they have acquired them honestly or inherited them legally... Do not say, "I am using what belongs to me." You are using what belongs to others. All the wealth of the world belongs to you and to the others in common, as the sun, air, earth and all the rest.[27]

In his encyclical *Mater et Magistra* (1961) Pope John XXIII quotes a statement made by Pius XII in 1941:

> The right to the private possession of material goods is admittedly a natural one; nevertheless, in the objective order established by God, the right to property cannot stand in the way of the axiomatic principle that "the goods which were created by God for all men should flow to all alike, according to the principles of justice and charity" (para. 43).

Mater et Magistra adds:

> Private ownership of property, including that of productive goods, is a natural right which the state cannot suppress. But it naturally entails a social obligation as well. It is a right which must be exercised not only for one's own personal benefit but also for the benefit of others (para. 19).

The second issue connected to irresponsible possession of economic power is economic democracy. We may note that while struggles for a democratization of business and industry have met with a certain degree of success in some local contexts (workers' councils, profit-sharing schemes, workers' representation on boards of directors), globally there have been no such achievements.

The frustration of the sense of Christian vocation. Oxford's concern was that "the only forms of employment open to many men and women – or the fact that none are open – prevent them from finding a sense of Christian vocation in their daily life". Unemployment creates a sense of *uselessness*. Indeed, Archbishop William Temple's seemingly self-evident truth, uttered in the years of the great depression, remains relevant: "the only answer to unemployment is employment".

A further concern relating to the notion of vocation is that many workers must produce shoddy or destructive goods. Vocation is frustrated when people are conscious only of working for the profit of the employer and their own wages while seeing no relation between their work and the public good. This point was already made by the Universal Christian Conference on Life and Work in Stockholm in 1925:

> Labour is not a commodity, but the contribution of persons to the economic process. The church must labour for and forward all measures which are clearly productive of personal value. The test which it should apply to policies and programmes is not that of economic efficiency but of personal welfare.[28]

Oxford's statements and norms formed the basis of the concept of the "responsible society", as developed by the first assembly of the World Council of Churches (Amsterdam 1948). The WCC's second assembly (Evanston 1954) proclaimed this notion as a major criterion to judge existing social orders and a standard to guide people in making concrete choices.[29]

Christian response in retrospect

It is striking in retrospect how pertinent Oxford's four major criticisms of the economic order in the industrialized world remain today. Moreover, it is noteworthy that, in regard to property, Oxford stressed "the underlying theological conviction that all the earth's resources are gifts of God to the human race and should be used with due and balanced consideration for the needs of present and future generations",[30] thus foreshadowing the churches' attention to the environmental crisis. As we have seen, several papal social encyclicals have made similar points.

But if the churches today stand in a solid tradition of conceptual, methodological and evaluative response to a world in economic disorder, institutional response is of course another matter. We have mentioned that *Rerum Novarum* received a follow-up in Christian trade unionism, which has often joined with trade unions originating from a socialist tradition to play a part in processes of reforming a capitalist economic order. Many churches and church organizations have offices and desks for globally oriented diaconia and social issues. Besides these forms of institutionalized solidarity on the part of the churches themselves, specific "Christian" organizations have been founded, including political parties. The latter, however, have demonstrated few differences from liberal and socialist parties:

> It would be incorrect to claim that in dealing with progress Christian political parties and social organizations, with respect to their practical policy, have displayed a style of their own, or that, in distinction from other such organizations, they occupied themselves intensively with the question of the *direction* of progress. Synthesis with the entire development of society is the mark of modern Christendom. For this reason both Christians and humanists are responsible for the presence of good and evil in the unfolding of the Western social order.[31]

Despite the development of a relatively coherent body of socio-economic thinking in both the Roman Catholic Church and the ecumenical movement, the extent to which one can speak of this response being incorporated into daily economic life remains doubtful. Christianity is still faced with the challenge of relevant and effective response to a world in economic disorder.

NOTES

[1] C. M. Elliott, "Ethical Issues in the Dynamics of Economic Development", in Denys Munby, ed., *Economic Growth in World Perspective*,

New York, Association, 1966, p.340.

[2] V. Obenhaus, *Ethics for an Industrial Age: A Christian Inquiry*, New York, Harper & Row, 1965, p.14.

[3] *Ibid.*, p.15. On the still-undecided debate over Weber's thesis see R.H. Tawney, *Religion and the Rise of Capitalism*, Harmondsworth, UK, Penguin, 1938, and R.H. Roberts, ed., *Religion and the Transformations of Capitalism: Comparative Approaches*, London and New York, Routledge, 1995. Bob Goudzwaard argues that "historically speaking, there is definitely a connection between capitalism and Calvinism through the intermediary of later Puritanism"; *Capitalism and Progress: A Diagnosis of Western Society,* Toronto, Wedge, 1979, p.8.

[4] A. van Leeuwen, *Christianity in World History: The Meeting of the Faiths of East and West*, London, Edinburgh House Press, 1964, p.403. His thesis that it was a "radical change in the very structure of Christianity" that sparked modernity was disputed by Paul Verghese (Paulos Mar Gregorios), who argued that van Leeuwen identified Christianity completely with its Greek branch and totally neglected the Hebrew-Judaic branch.

[5] Quoted by Denys Munby, *Christianity and Economic Problems*, London, Macmillan, 1956, p.238.

[6] Goudzwaard, *op. cit.*, pp.35, 153, 244. He argues that the modern notion of progress in terms of economic growth and technological development was sparked by the Renaissance, deism, natural law and utilitarianism rather than by a radical change in the structure of Christianity, as argued by van Leeuwen. Indeed, he criticizes the lack of an adequate Christian response to such civilizational developments.

[7] *The Church and the Disorder of Society*: an ecumenical study prepared under the auspices of the World Council of Churches, London, SCM Press, 1948, p.177.

[8] Quoted in *Economics: A Matter of Faith*, a study document of the Commission of the Churches on Participation in Development, Geneva, WCC, 1988, p.2.

[9] On the question of *status confessionis* see J. Barndt and S. Schroeder, "Confessing Christ and Resisting Capitalism: Is the Prevailing Economic Order a *Status Confessionis*?", *ibid.*, pp.31-46. This issue has been a matter of continued discussion within the World Alliance of Reformed Churches (which took a similar stand on the issue of apartheid), especially since its general council meeting in Debrecen, Hungary, in August 1997.

[10] Cf. Juan Carlos Scannone, *Teología de la Liberación y Doctrina Social de la Iglesia*, Madrid and Buenos Aires, Ed. Cristiandad and Ed. Gua-

dalupe, 1987, pp. 149-54.

[11] M.-D. Chenu, *La "Doctrine Sociale" de l'Eglise comme Idéologie*, Paris, Desclée, 1979, ch. 6.

[12] J.K. Galbraith, in *National Catholic Reporter*, 27 May 1988, p.13.

[13] Gustavo Gutiérrez, "Las cosas nuevas de hoy: Una relectura de la Rerum Novarum", *Páginas*, Vol. 16, no.110, 1991, pp.10-12.

[14] In *Quadragesimo Anno*, Pius XI wrote that "if the class struggle abstains from enmities and mutual hatred, it gradually changes into an honest discussion of differences founded on a desire for justice" (para. 114); cf. *Laborem Exercens*, paras 11-15, and *Centesimus Annus*, para. 14.

[15] Cf. Gutiérrez, *loc. cit.;* O. von Nell-Breuning, *Gerechtigkeit und Freiheit: Grundzüge katholischer Soziallehre*, Vienna, Europaverlag, 1980; C. Boff, "Doctrina social de la Iglesia y teología de la liberación", in *Concilium*, no. 170, 1981, pp.468-76; V. Zsifkovits, "Grundprinzipien der katholischen Soziallehre", *Theologisch-Praktische Quartalschrift*, Vol. 138, no.1, 1990, pp.16-25.

[16] In C. Mulholland, ed., *Ecumenical Reflections on Political Economy*, Geneva, WCC, 1988, p.73.

[17] Cf. Adam Smith, *An Inquiry into the Nature and Causes of the Wealth of Nations* (1776), repr. London, George Routledge & Son, 1900, Book III, ch.1.

[18] R. Heilbroner, *21st-Century Capitalism*, New York, W. W. Norton, 1993, p.155.

[19] *Ibid.*, p.42.

[20] R.H. Tawney, *The Acquisitive Society*, New York, Harvest Books, 1920, p.31.

[21] P. A. Wicksteed, *The Common Sense of Political Economy*, London, 1949, p.174.

[22] Cf. B. de Gaay Fortman, "Is Socialism Possible?", *Sociological Analysis*, Vol. 1, no.1, Feb.-March 1998.

[23] Quoted in *Economics: A Matter of Faith*, p.4.

[24] J.R. Commons, *The Legal Foundations of Capitalism*, New York, 1924.

[25] D.H. Robertson, *The Control of Industry*, Cambridge, Cambridge U.P., 1933, p.89.

[26] In a short work entitled *Naboth*; quoted by W.J. Walsh & J.P. Langan, "Patristic Social Consciousness: The Church and the Poor", in J.G. Haughey, ed., *The Faith That Does Justice: Examining the Christian Sources for Social Change*, Ramsey, NJ, Paulist Press, 1977, p.128.

[27] Quoted in *ibid.*, notes 55-56.

[28] In Mulholland, *op. cit.*, p.30.

[29] H.M. de Lange, *De Gestalte van een Verantwoordelijke Maatschappij*, Amsterdam, Ten Have, 1966, p.249.
[30] John C. Bennett, "Breakthrough in Ecumenical Social Ethics", *The Ecumenical Review*, Vol. 40, no.2, April 1988, p.145.
[31] B. Goudzwaard, *op. cit.*, p.xxx.

4. Can Global Capitalism Survive?

Man's disorder is inescapably manifest in every aspect of the world's life today.

World Council of Churches 1948
Amsterdam Assembly (1948)

Communism was meant to be more than just an alternative to capitalism; it was seen as its *successor*. However, this system which the Russian Orthodox philosopher Nicolas Berdyaev called a "twisted realization of Christian social truth" did not survive. "Real existing socialism" could be managed only in combination with political dictatorship. This implied a fundamental lack of flexibility. Its economies were thoroughly inefficient,[1] and when the time came to restructure them–*perestroika*–it was realized that such a major exercise would not be possible without opening up society to criticism: *glasnost*. This in fact meant the end of Leninism in the sense of an avant-garde party's monopoly on truth. Not surprisingly, the whole system collapsed.

In contrast, capitalism has survived. Its comparative advantage lies in flexibility based on its constant susceptibility to economic-political compromise. But this depends on continuous challenges transforming the contradictions of the system into actual opposition, social struggle and reform. The collapse of real existing socialism, however, has left capitalism without challenging alternative visions. Moreover, as was shown in chapter 2, capitalism today has acquired a *global* character. Thus, the question is whether global capitalism can survive without socialism. Finding an answer to that question first requires some insight into capitalist economic-political compromise.

The "social market economy"

Despite predictions from different angles of its downfall–Marx for reasons of increasing misery; Schumpeter on the ground that the dominance of individualist materialism would destroy the socio-cultural environment it requires – the capitalist mode of production has endured the times. Unlike authoritarian socialism, capitalism in combination with pluralist democracy has shown both flexibility and reformability. Time and again, protest and dissent have been transformed into actual opposition, collective action and reform. In particular, we can identify four structurally corrective mechanisms to "free" market economies: the strong state, the welfare state, the responsible company and social cohesion within a strong civil society.

The strong state. The need for a strong state was already emphasized by Adam Smith in 1776. The state has the duties of protecting the society against external aggression, establishing an "exact administration of justice" and arranging the provision of collective goods and services. Particularly to be emphasized is the need for properly functioning legal infrastructures – nowadays considered to be part of good governance. In addition to its role in providing collective goods and services, the modern state must embark on public regulation in regard to natural monopolies and industries with unstable markets. Protection of the environment requires public ways and means to deal with "externalities" – that is, the effects of economic activities whose costs are not attributed to those who take the decisions. For example, acid rain, resulting from bio-industry, may destroy forests and thus, among other things, affect the tourism industry.

The welfare state. A welfare state accepts responsibility for the welfare of its citizens. A typical feature is social insurance offering protection to people in economically weak positions such as unemployed workers, disabled persons, the sick and the aged. A social safety net based on minimum welfare should protect people who have no alternative source of income against absolute and relative poverty. This also implies transferring income from the general taxpayer to the less privileged in order to reduce socio-economic inequality. After the depression in the Western industrialized countries in the 1930s it was also accepted that the state should attempt through its fiscal and other policies to secure full employment.

The responsible company. The mid-20th century saw the appearance of books such as *The Responsible Company*,[2] which argued that continuity, rather than maximizing short-term profits, was the guiding corporate principle. Naturally, profitability remains a *sine qua non* in private business, but management must be equally concerned with such other norms as good public, industrial and human relations.[3] The latter might be seen as a response to Archbishop of Cantberbury William Temple's remark that what workers need most is "social fellowship".

Social cohesion. Here we come back to Schumpeter's prediction of the end of capitalism. Without moral commitment, he argued, capitalism would not survive. The pursuit of private interests in the economy must be supported by a focus on wider interests in socio-cultural relations. Indeed, capitalism appears to coincide with social stability particularly when it is embedded in societies based on social bonding, trust, affection and a shared sacred meaning.[4]

The deficit of global politics

The processes of economic and financial globalization have seriously affected all four of these areas which have given capitalism its political and socio-cultural embedding. The global economy lacks a strong political institution and there are no corrective mechanisms to global inequality. Having lost its embedding in specific communities, the global corporation has detached itself from the human interest. Finally, as we have seen, the downside of globalization is exclusion, leading inevitably to processes of social disintegration.

Global political disorder. The lack of control in the economic disorder of the world today manifests itself particularly in the impotence of its political centre. There is a striking contrast between economic globalization and the absence of global political control. Although it is obvious that global markets should be supplemented by supranational institutional arrangements, global governance is almost entirely lacking. The international economic order still shows the major traits of colonial exploitation; and corrective mechanisms are almost entirely absent.

Although the founding of the United Nations as a universal intergovernmental organization for peace and development has been characterized as one of the few "breakthroughs in twentieth century politics, regardless of how successful it has been in practice",[5] world government remains an illusion. This has serious consequences in a time of economic globalization. While processes of social development could correct social injustices in a national context in order to assure socio-political stability, globally such mechanisms are lacking. Hence, nation-states and the systems of treaties among them remain of utmost importance. Unfortunately, economic and financial globalization seem to be weakening rather than reinforcing the state. In this way the sustainability of the capitalist system is affected.

Growing environmental insecurity. In the broadest sense security has to do with safety in the face of the many threats people come up against in their lives. Safety means protection against disaster. If you fall into the water, for example, a life-belt will keep you afloat and safe. In addition, security means a minimization of risks. Thus, it is important to take measures that will prevent you from falling into the water in the first place. Security thus implies both prevention and protection. It means freedom from disaster, fear, attack and violent disruption. This encompasses many different aspects, among which the environment is playing a more and more important role.

The narrow interpretation of threats to environmental security highlights the danger of inter- and intra-state violence as a result of environmental and resource conflicts. An illustration is the Horn of Africa, where lack of sustainable development is regarded as a major cause of armed conflict.[6] A more controversial interpretation extends the idea of environmental security to the more general thesis which conceives environmental degradation as a direct threat to human survival, even without the immediate prospect of armed conflict.[7] While this broadening of the understanding of threats and vulnerabilities is to be welcomed, little is gained if including environmental concerns in the concept of security must be seen as a sacrifice "to the jealous deity of sovereignty".[8]

Despite recent attention to insecurity from within, security is still construed primarily in terms of the concern of sovereign states with external threats and vulnerabilities. In this respect the mandate of the United Nations Conference on Environment and Development in Rio de Janeiro (1992) was rather ambiguous. In fact, the resolution of the UN general assembly from which the "Earth Summit" emanated stressed the sovereign right of states to develop their own resources pursuant to their own policies – so long as these activities do not cause environmental damage to areas beyond their jurisdiction. Thus, the challenge of environmental security is set in the context of a world of sovereign states – precisely the setting in which the environmental crises developed. Falk already expressed doubts on this score in 1971 in *The Endangered Planet*:

> A world of sovereign states is unable to cope with endangered-planet problems... Such a system exhibits only a modest capacity for international cooperation and coordination. The distribution of power and authority, as well as the organization of human effort, is overwhelmingly guided by the selfish drives of nations.[9]

The seriousness of the threats and vulnerabilities involved means that ensuring environmental security requires some rather hard decisions. However, the spaces in which these decisions must be taken are still determined by a world of sovereign states. Principle 15 of the Rio Declaration specifies that each state must apply the *precautionary principle* in estimating the risks related to its own environmental behaviour; but the general preoccupation with economic growth endorsed by the same declaration makes it highly unlikely that any state will do this honestly, wholeheartedly and with full acceptance of the consequences for the immediate "human welfare" of its own citizens. Environmental choices are based on perceptions of risks and protection of vested interests.[10] Not surprisingly, what we note in practice is not so much the avoidance of risk as the *redistribution* of risk.

Indeed, it is the redistribution of risk rather than the redistribution of wealth and resources that now dominates the international agenda. Thus, the South is supposed to mitigate the effects of environmental threats and vulnerabilities from the North in such areas as carbon dioxide emissions, energy supply and global pollution. Such a climate ensured in advance the failure of the Rio follow-up meetings in New York (1997) and Manila (1998).

The implementation of Agenda 21 – Rio's blueprint for a global partnership in handling the major environmental crises – suffers from three principal defects:

– There is insufficient recognition that "because the solutions to the problems of the environment must be global they present an unprecedented challenge to concepts of national sovereignty".[11]
– Security is detached from peace and with that from a concern for right relations among people. Thus, security and prevention replace the elimination of poverty as objectives of North-South "cooperation". Environmental security should be linked not only to other aspects of security but also to a norm like *justice*.[12]
– The notion of sustainable development, in which contemporary strategies for environmental security are rooted, remains a primarily *economic* concept. The Brundtland Report, which launched this concept, noted that "meeting essential needs depends in part on achieving full growth potential, and sustainable development clearly requires economic growth in places where such needs are not being met".[13]

Nor did Agenda 21 address the dialectics of economy and ecology. As Rasmussen has noted:

> There is a serious tension between the means proposed to achieve sustainable development (the reform of trade, aid and finance of Chapter 2) and the goals necessary to achieve such development (combatting poverty and changing consumption patterns outlined in Chapters 3 and 4). It is, in fact, likely that the means utterly frustrate the end. If that is so the survival ethics fails. Development as a concept remains anchored in the very strategies by which current economic growth was achieved, the kind of growth which is now the bane of ecological well-being. It is rooted in post-World War II economic expansion and continues within the framework of globalized capitalist economy.[14]

Social disintegration. Korten describes the unbridled operation of money as the primary driving force of the world today as a kind of *colonization*:

> What we are experiencing might best be described as a case of money colonizing life. To accept this absurd distortion of human

institutions and purpose should be considered nothing less than an act of collective, suicidal insanity.[15]

Again and again, modern types of "progress" based on new technologies have driven substantial numbers of people off their land–through the "green revolution" for example–and out of their jobs. Seldom if ever in such situations have there been adequate institutional mechanisms to support humane processes of transition for the people affected. Those facing the consequences of such marginalization and exclusion do not always quietly accept their fate. The phenomenon of regional and even global migration has had an enormous impact on the fabric of many societies. Indeed, Korten speaks of *social disintegration* as part of the "threefold crisis" of humanity:

> Economic globalization has come at a heavy price. In the name of modernization we are creating dysfunctional societies that are breeding pathological behaviour – violence, extreme competitiveness, suicide, drug abuse, greed, and environmental degradation–on every hand... The threefold crisis of deepening poverty, environmental destruction and social disintegration is a manifestation of this dysfunction.[16]

Thus we are brought back to Schumpeter's still unfulfilled prediction of an end to capitalism through its own ideological impact. Finally, the capitalist frame of mind, "after having destroyed the moral authority of so many other institutions, would turn against its own".[17] As soon as enough people learn "the utilitarian lesson" and acquire "the habit of weighing the individual advantages and disadvantages of any prospective course of action", the whole socio-cultural order that must sustain the system, including the values of family life, will be in jeopardy.[18] The real threat, then, is that the "economic motive" in its individualist-materialist version permeates and dominates all spheres of life.

Capitalism in place of the state. We have seen that capitalism needs a strong state, not just to establish law and order and provide for collective goods but also to handle major problems which the market cannot resolve. We mentioned the challenges of externalities (including ecological issues), the fundamental instability of certain markets and an economic policy aiming at full employment. Today, however, the role of the state seems to be weakened rather than strengthened. We would identify two principal causes of this apparent impotence of the post-modern capitalist state. The first has to do with the state as such, the second with the quality of politics.

The impossibility of socialism is rooted in what has been called the "principals-agents" problem. In short, why would the "agents" – the people – follow the directives of the "principals" – the avant-garde party? In practice, ideological persuasion has proved to be inadequate; and all systems of real existing socialism had to be maintained with the support of various forms of coercion and repression. In the case of a capitalist state, however, the major question is: "Who are its principals?"[19] The answers given to this question by both neo-classical economists (the consumers or the citizens) and Marxists (the capitalists) are too simplistic.

From an historical perspective, in many capitalist countries a state appears to emerge which is not entirely subject to the interests of private business. Depending on the strength of pluralist democracy and the positions of political parties committed to redistribution and structural change, the role of the state has shown more nuance. Moreover, "private business" could neither be seen as only "capital" or only responding to consumer interests. To use the image of Yvon Gattaz, liberal capitalism must function like a soccer game, with an impartial umpire who can be relied upon to stick to the rules.

Unfortunately, the post-modern capitalist state does not conform to this picture. Capital has become incredibly mobile, and it penetrates everywhere. If a more or less autonomous state was ever accepted by the forces of capital, this is certainly not the case today. The tendency is twofold: (1) what used to be regarded as public is now considered private, with *privatization* as a key slogan; (2) there are increasing attempts everywhere to buy the agents of the state. Michel Albert has discerned three ages of capitalism: 1791 – capitalism *against* the state; 1891 – capitalism encapsulated *by* the state; 1991 – capitalism *in place of* the state.[20] Given that the realm of capital already had the upper hand, the realm of the state is in jeopardy today more than ever.

Democracy in peril. The second cause of the contemporary predicament of the capitalist state lies in the operation of democracy. While electoral defeat could be seen as the major constraint on the powers of the principals of a state, elections have now become subordinated to financial manipulation.[21] A new seat in the US Senate is likely to cost between US$10 and 20 million. An American journalist has pointed to two ways a citizen can run for such office:

> The first is by taking what are euphemistically called campaign contributions, bribes in plain English, from corporations and PACs [political action committees], on the understanding that you'll do what they want later on. The second is by being both inordinately rich and narcissistic enough to blow $28 million of your own money in the quest for power.

Most of this money is necessary to get access to the mass media. At the same time, this observer notes, network television appears to have abandoned any attempt to cover elections in terms of issues – that is, the presentation and comparison of different approaches to current problems in the public and political arena:

> More and more, network political coverage treats politics as a kind of gladiatorial sport, obsessively asking who's losing, who's winning, and failing to explore the nature of issues. But conflict and prosecution are not necessarily the whole story. Having sown this wind, we now reap the whirlwind of an absurdly caricatured polity, under whose stresses the traditional American genius for compromise, which is the heart of a pluralist democracy, is breaking down.

If there is one issue that does still penetrate to the electorate it is lower taxes. Although major problems will remain insoluble without increased public finance, even in a relatively progressive country like the Netherlands all the major political parties promise voters a reduction of the collective tax burden on businesses and individuals.[22] To withstand the trend towards populism of this type, democracy needs strong citizens who are able to see through the cheap and inconsistent promises that are made. Unfortunately, the mass media which trivialize the electoral system are also not oriented to creating strong and aware citizens. It should be noted that while a strong state requires strong voluntary associations (civil society), a strong democracy requires strong citizens.

Global civilization at the crossroads. This analysis leads to two concluding observations. The first is that capitalism cannot survive without strong institutional support of a socio-cultural nature. The capitalism which heretofore provided considerable stability was corporate or organized capitalism, with more or less responsible corporations and a state more or less above private business, reasonably fulfilling its duties of government. At the end of the 20th century, we are witnessing serious threats to existing types of relatively sustainable capitalism. Most threatening is the globalization of capitalism as a primarily economic and financial process without any significant development of global political and social counterforces. While in a national context capitalism could be "socialized", no degree whatsoever of socialization of the international economic order can be noticed.

Second, the threefold global crisis of ecological destruction, deepening poverty and social disintegration is well known. Yet, as Vaclav Havel has said, "humankind does nothing to avert the threats about which it knows so much". He goes on:

> It is my deep conviction that the only option is for something to change in the sphere of the spirit, in the actual attitude of man towards the world and his understanding of himself and his place in the overall order of existence. It cannot suffice to invent new machines, new regulations, new institutions. It is necessary to understand differently and more perfectly the true purpose of our existence on this earth and of our deeds. Only such new understanding will allow the development of new models of behaviour, new scales of value and life objectives, and through this means finally attach a new spirit and new meaning also to the specific regulations, treaties and institutions.[23]

Can global capitalism survive? Without global change of a civilizational nature it is unlikely to. More than half a century ago Schumpeter already noticed a "tendency towards another civilization that slowly works deep down below".[24] However, that new civilization is not yet perceptible. After the betrayal of "the god of progress" and his prophet of economic growth,[25] could it be based on a spirit other than unrestrained materialism, a worldview which characterized both capitalism and socialism? Before tackling that question and searching for new civilizational perspectives, we should look first at current constraints on a Christian impact on a world in economic disorder.

NOTES

1 The system produced enormous waste. For example, between 15 and 20 percent of the natural gas in the former USSR was lost to leakage, compared to a negligible percentage in Western industrialized countries. Similar losses existed in oil production and agriculture. Obsolete production techniques created severe pollution, threatening environmental catastrophe, and stocks were larger than the gross domestic product and more than four times what is usual in Western industrialized economies. According to the "Russia Survey" in *The Economist*, 5 Dec. 1992, p.10, if "all the raw materials that Russia produces were sold abroad, the country would earn twice as much as its present total GDP". Since raw material output is included in the GDP, Russian industry was in effect "subtracting, not adding, value to the raw materials it consumed".

2 G. Goyder, *The Responsible Company*, Oxford, Basil Blackwell, 1961; cf. P. Kuin, *Ordening als Maatschappelijk Verschijnsel*, Haarlem, 1938.

3 Cf. B. de Gaay Fortman, *Theory of Competition Policy: A Confrontation of Economic, Political and Legal Principles*, Amsterdam, North Holland, 1966, pp.123f.

4 Cf. F. Fukuyama, *Trust: The Social Virtues and the Creation of Prosperity*, New York, The Free Press, 1995; and D. Korten, *op. cit.*, p.261.

5 B. Bassin, "What Role for the United Nations in World Economic and Social Development?", paper for the UNDP Stockholm Roundtable on Global Change, 22-24 July 1994, p.1.

6 Cf. R.K. Molvaer, "Environmentally Induced Conflicts: A Discussion Based on Studies from the Horn of Africa", *Bulletin of Peace Proposals*, Vol. 22, no.2, 1991, pp.175-88.

7 Cf. M.S. Soroos, "Global Change, Environmental Security and the Prisoner's Dilemma", *Journal of Peace Research*, Vol. 31, no.3, 1994, pp.317-32.

8 J. Stoett, "The Environmental Enlightenment: Security Analysis Meets Ecology", *Coexistence*, Vol. 31, 1994, p.127.

[9] Quoted by Stoett, *ibid.*, p.135.

[10] J. Stoett, "Global Environmental Security, Energy Resources and Planning", *Futures*, Vol. 26, no.7, 1994, p.745.

[11] Newman, "The New Diplomatic Agenda: Are Governments Ready?", *International Affairs*, Vol. 65, no. 1, 1989, p.35.

[12] Justice is a norm pertaining to relations among human beings and thus differs from norms regarding the relationship between people and the environment (such as ecosystem health or "integrity of creation"). The term "eco-justice" confuses the issue; the challenge lies in simultaneous realization of norms rather than mixing them together.

[13] World Committee of Experts on Environment and Development, *Our Common Future*, Oxford, Oxford U.P., 1987, p.44.

[14] In N. J. Brown and P. Quiblier, eds, *Ethics and Agenda 21: Moral Implications of a Global Consensus*, New York, United Nations, 1994, p.55.

[15] *When Corporations Rule the World*, p.247.

[16] *Ibid.*, pp.261f.

[17] J. A. Schumpeter, *Capitalism, Socialism and Democracy*, New York, Harper, 1947, p.143.

[18] *Ibid.*, p.157.

[19] Pitelis, "On the Nature of the Capitalist State", *Political Economy*, Vol. 6, no. 1, 1994, p.73.

[20] Michel Albert, *Capitalisme contre capitalisme*, Paris, Editions du Seuil, 1991, pp.292-97.

[21] Pitelis, *op. cit.*, pp.98f.

[22] The Netherlands (like Germany, Switzerland, Scandinavia and to a certain extent Japan) has been described in terms of the so-called Rhineland capitalism, in which the degree of socialization of certain business functions is much higher than in the US and the UK, so that these countries have faced less socio-economic marginalization and less socio-cultural polarization. Today, however, they are also facing postmodern developments affecting the socio-cultural embedding of capitalism.

[23] From his opening statement for Forum 2000, Prague, 1997 (unpublished), p.3.

[24] *Op. cit.*, p.163.

[25] Cf. Bob Goudzwaard, *Capitalism and Progress*, p.249.

5. The Paralysis of Christianity in Responding to Global Moral Issues

For Christian ethics focused mainly on sexuality and everything that had to be prohibited, didn't it? Augustine and Calvin took a stand in regard to politics, but it has been a long time since a good Christian social ethics was presented. Christianity has offered politics little support.

H.J. Heering

The social ethics of the churches has been shaped in response to historical crises. It grows out of a twofold encounter – on the one hand between the church, capitalism and communism as economic systems; on the other hand between the church, liberalism and socialism as socio-political ideologies.[1] In the previous chapters we have seen something of the critical character of social doctrine with regard to each of these systems and ideologies. But the churches' apparent lack of relevance to the development of future perspectives on global civilization remains problematic. Major institutions in society neglect or disregard socio-economic orientations emerging from the churches' social teaching. Many individual Christians partially or completely ignore any Christian orientation in economic matters. When the churches' stand on social ethical issues does come to public attention, as in the United Nations' world conferences on population (Cairo) and women (Beijing), it has generated a good deal of debate and controversy as a result of ambiguities in the Holy See's position.[2] How is the value conflict between social ethics, with its remarkable socio-economic directions, and sexual ethics, with its censuring of contraception, to be explained? How should we understand the limited success of the Catholic Church in having its teaching authority followed in practical and institutional socio-economic life?

A few obvious factors contributing to this situation come immediately to mind. For one thing, despite the challenging nature of the issues addressed, the social teaching of the churches seems rather abstract. Some would also suspect it of a hidden ideology. And as we have already suggested, Catholic social teaching in particular tends to be so heavily associated with its dissenting positions on issues of sexual morality and birth control that attention to what it has to say on socio-economic questions is severely undermined.

Behind these general explanations are more substantial factors inherent in the conceptual structure and methods of the social teaching of the churches. In this chapter we shall look briefly at some of these elements.

The "Third Way" dilemma

Amidst strikingly clear developments in Catholic social teaching, some aspects appear to remain in an ambiguous immobility. A case in point is what has been called its "third way" paralysis regarding alternative types of economic order. In its tradition of social teaching the Catholic Church has never proposed concrete models of or blueprints for society. The social encyclicals consider the elaboration of such models to be beyond the competence of the Church. Rather, this is the responsibility of social and political actors, depending on different concrete historical situations (cf. *Centesimus Annus*, para. 5). However, the encyclicals explicitly contrast Catholic social teaching with the geopolitics of both liberal capitalism and Marxist socialism. The communist East and the capitalist West are held equally responsible for all the evil in the world (cf. *Sollicitudo Rei Socialis*, paras 20ff.). Their political polarization was seen as not only aggravating the economic division between North and South but also leading the entire world to self-destruction.

In reaction to such a "third-way" critique, Paul VI's encyclical *Octogesima Adveniens* characterizes social teaching as a normative framework which identifies key values and establishes criteria for discernment and judgment, thus entering into dialogue with every social system. John Paul II has been even more explicit in his rejection of a "third way", describing social teaching as a guide which can be used to assess the limits of any social system and provide direction for change and reform. This rejection of a third way, along with the explicit decision to speak out for the poor and to identify with those who are struggling for social justice, implies a radical socio-economic position. However, the remarkable ambiguities in the Catholic Church's stance in other areas generate much genuine misunderstanding and dispute. Regrettably, this also leads to misreading and biased discrediting of specific socio-economic orientations. This constitutes one of the major difficulties in the reception of social teaching.

The precise demarcation between moral and political orientations is indeed a major problem facing social teaching. It is of course impossible to mark clearly the frontier between ethics and politics, especially since the social teaching of the Church does not limit itself to individual ethics but also addresses the collective responsibility of groups, peoples and humanity. Academic economic circles have identified a further major problem: a theoretical deficit which results from an approach which focuses on the distribution of goods while not seriously taking into account their *production*.[3]

However, in his analysis of *Centesimus Annus*, Houtart rejects any interpretation which would suggest a "third way" dilemma. He even notes an important difference in the Church's evaluation of real capitalism and real existing socialism: the former, he says, is condemned for its abuses and is therefore reformable, while the latter is condemned in its essence and is thus unable to be amended.[4]

Globalization and the quest for a Christian humanism

Recent social teaching has not yet come fully to terms with the fact that the capitalist economic system has achieved global proportions. While in many countries the old *capitalisme sauvage* had been replaced by a new form of *capitalisme civilisé*, the world economic system manifests a new global dimension of inequality and injustice.[5] Already at the beginning of the 1980s *Laborem Exercens* had pointed in this direction:

> While in the past the "class" question was especially highlighted as the centre of this issue, in more recent times it is the "world" question that is emphasized. Thus, not only the sphere of class is taken into consideration but also the world sphere of inequality and

> injustice, and as a consequence, not only the class dimension but also the world dimension of the tasks involved in the path towards the achievement of justice in the modern world (para. 9).

Several years later *Sollicitudo Rei Socialis* not only linked the "social question" to issues of global development, but also stated that this assumes an international dimension in contemporary development discussions, especially in the form of "limits to growth" (paras 26, 34, 47).

Pope John Paul II's goal is undoubtedly much more ambitious than just responding to processes of globalization and development. He is rather seeking to capitalize on the institutional continuity of the Catholic Church and its social, cultural, ecclesial and theological reforms to find a new role as a great moral power in a globalizing world. Focusing on anthropological teaching and socio-ethical orientations, John Paul II is not looking for socio-economic answers in conformity with Christian principles; he is rather trying to formulate a "Christian humanism" as the basis for protecting human dignity. This Christian humanism is presented as an appropriate response to all contemporary socio-economic problems. But it is doubtful that global humanity and global civilization could be considered as receptive to a universal appeal to Christian humanism. We shall return to this question of Christianity's place amidst a plurality of world religions in our final chapter.

The lack of internal application of social teaching

One ambiguity of Catholic social teaching is the Church's apparent inability to apply it to its own internal organization. Although John Paul II insisted in *Centesimus Annus* that the Catholic Church is more aware than ever that the credibility of its social message has more to do with the testimony of its works than the coherence and internal logic of the message itself, major discrepancies still appear in practice.

The document *Justice in the World* (1971) stated that evangelical and prophetic witness requires the Church to administer its own goods in such a way that the gospel is proclaimed to the poor. The well-known letter of the US bishops on *Economic Justice for All* (1986) stated that "the Church cannot redeem the world from the deadening effects of sin and injustice unless it is working to remove sin and injustice in its own life and institutions" (para. 24). In this light the pope's recent nominations, especially in third world countries, of conservative bishops who are notorious defenders of the status quo and indifferent or even hostile to the new social teaching can hardly be regarded as consistent with the Church's position on economic affairs. Moreover, it seems questionable to involve only men in the production of documents on social teaching, marginalizing women already in the process of drafting.

The issue of reconciling the Church's material wealth with its social teaching is illuminated by a remark of Cyprian, bishop of Carthage in the mid-third century, who reflected on the consequences of the long years of peace which had allowed the Church to accumulate its own property:

> Gone was the devotion of bishops to the service of God, gone was the clergy's faithful integrity, gone the generous compassion for the needy, gone all the discipline in our behaviour... Too many bishops... left their sees, abandoned their people, and toured the market in other territories on the outlook for profitable deals.[6]

Lack of ecumenical cooperation in social ethics

Despite the often-cited insight of the Universal Christian Conference on Life and Work (Stockholm 1925) that "the world is too strong for a divided church", Catholic social teaching is not made in union with other churches, even though the same issues face everyone in one world and, as African theologian John Pobee once observed, injustice and violence do not show a different face when committed against Protestants as distinct from Roman Catholics. Indeed, it would be a greater witness to the one God to have the churches speak with one voice on social issues. Konrad Raiser, general secretary of the WCC, welcomes the broadening of doctrinal convergence and agreement between different Christian traditions but goes on to point to the difficulty of ecumenical cooperation in the area of ethics:

> Profound differences of moral and ethical orientation are giving rise to new lines of division, both within and between the churches. Whereas the methods of dialogue have been refined in the field of

theology and doctrine, the churches seem to lack even the basic elements of a common language where the ethics of life and procreation or of human sexuality are concerned. If I am not mistaken, many of the contemporary frontier issues facing the ecumenical movement arise precisely in this area of moral and ethical reflection.[7]

Authoritative character and intercultural cooperation

Another constraint arises out of the tension between the claim to teaching authority and its limitation in practical application to society. Explaining the authoritative character of Catholic social teaching, the Latin American Bishops' Conference (CELAM) speaks of the living memory of the Church's social and historical experience, which retains the universal and infinite in diverse and changing realities.[8] Yet, why should it be exclusively *Catholic* social teaching that embodies the memory of the past? A global orientation on basic ethics in regard to the global economy requires democratic forms of (inter)ecclesial and intercultural cooperation. In this context, Diarmuid Martin, of the Pontifical Commission Justice and Peace, writes:

> Every culture is able to express human rights in their entirety, and must be challenged to do that within the wealth of cultural traditional experience that it has...[9]
>
> For me the full respect of cultures is not to deny the faults that exist in my culture or in anybody else's culture, but also to recognize the values of cultures. I am a universalist in many ways. But I believe in a universality in which all cultures and the richness of cultures can bring their contributions with a tremendous variety. Otherwise our universalism would be very empty and probably dangerous.[10]

Moreover, the claim to authoritative intervention relates to the specificity of social teaching as an *ethical discipline* in a plurality of cultures. The ethical orientation and its claim to universality ought to be explained by way of a critical recognition of the values and norms of different cultures and religions. The ethical foundations for a global orientation might be further developed through voluntary and equitable participation by different cultures and religions – another issue to which we shall turn in the final chapter.

Lack of integration

In conclusion, there seems to be a lack of integration of social teaching within the Catholic Church's moral teaching in general. Particularly in regard to specific moral questions (abortion, euthanasia, birth control) the social magisterium claims absolute authority. Yet sexual ethics cannot be separated from the social and economic conditions in which people live nor from questions of equity and equality, justice and rights. The obvious discrepancy between the absolute way of dealing with morality in sexual matters and the balanced approach of principles and guidelines in regard to socio-economic issues is a major complicating factor. Regarding social and economic life the Church rightly warns against any attempt to absolutize or construct deterministic models. Catholic social teaching undermines its own credibility in its treatment of sexual morality. A renewed and more integrated ethical basis of social teaching should be regarded as a necessary condition for the structural changes required to attain a sustainable and just international order.

NOTES

1 F. Houtart, "Théologie de la Libération et Doctrine Sociale de l'Eglise: Une Perspective Sociologique" (unpublished lecture at the University of Laval, Québec), March 1996, p.7.

2 Cf. B. Klein Goldewijk, "Renewed Ethical Basis for a Sustainable and Just International Order", in *Population and Development Controversy: Ethics and Global Culture*, Oegstgeest, NL, Cebemo, 1994, pp.5-32.

3 W. Kerber, "Katholische Soziallehre und Wirtschaftswissenschaft", in K. Gabriel, W. Klein and W. Krämer, eds, *Die gesellschaftliche Verantwortung der Kirche: Zur Enzyklika Sollicitudo Rei Socialis*, Düsseldorf, Patmos Verlag, 1988, pp.37f.

4 *Houtart, op. cit.*, p.10.

5 *Ibid.*, p.8.

6 Quoted in W. Walsh and J. P. Langan, "Patristic Social Consciousness", *loc. cit.*, p.123.

7 K. Raiser, "Fifty Years of Ecumenical Formation: Where Are We? Where Are We Going?", *The Ecumenical Review*, Vol. 48, no.4, Oct. 1996, pp.440-51.

[8] CELAM, *Fe Cristiana y Compromiso social: Elementos para una Reflexión sobre América Latina a la Luz de la Doctrina Social de la Iglesia*, Buenos Aires, 1983, pp.149-54.

[9] Msgr D. Martin, "Tensions Between Human Rights and Cultural Traditions", in B. Klein Goldewijk, ed., *Human Rights and Gender Equality*, Oegstgeest, NL, Vastenaktie-Cebemo, 1996, p.8.

[10] B. Klein Goldewijk, "Human Rights, Cultural Pluriformity and Gender Issues", in *Human Rights and Gender Equality*, p.46.

6. In Search of Civilizational Perspectives

What could change the tendencies of today's civilization? What could really stop the perpetual motion which we have not been able to control so far?

Vaclav Havel (1997)

There is an increasing tendency not to approach the global predicament on the basis of ideological perspectives or worldviews but rather in a certain *mood*. Let us look at four prevalent moods today.

1. *Liberal optimism.* Francis Fukuyama launched the idea of the "end of ideology" – a conviction that the combination of a market economy with liberal democracy provides the ultimate civilizational perspective – in a famous article published just after the fall of the Berlin wall.[1] On this view liberal democracy has not only triumphed over all other ideologies but has put an end to history, seen as a process of confrontations between ideologies. That Fukuyama's optimism about the world coming after the "end of history" is not unlimited is shown by his use, in the title of his subsequent book, of the expression "the last man".[2] This expression was earlier used by Friedrich Nietzsche, one of the first writers to lose faith in the future of Western modernity. Yet Fukuyama does embrace liberal democracy – born, as he sees it, in the womb of Western civilization – as crucial for the future of global humanity.[3]

2. *Liberal pessimism.* In the light of human history since the end of the cold war, this kind of optimism seems remote indeed. On the contrary, there appears to be a rapidly growing concern with the spiritual roots of the global crises, namely neo-liberalism. Insofar as this ideology still represents the spirit of our age, it manifests itself less often as optimism than as pessimism. The current liberal-pessimist mood approaches development problems as problems of the South to whose solution the North can hardly contribute.[4] Indeed, liberal pessimism regards deepening poverty, intra-state col-

lective violence, environmental degradation and social disintegration as phenomena beyond human control, at least from a global perspective.

3. *Social optimism.* On the opposite side of the spectrum we find a mood that appears rather dominant in United Nations circles and is expressed in statements about what "we" should do, establish and create in order to change the global (dis)order.[5] What is left unclear in such expressions of social optimism is what exactly *will* be done and who is the "we" who will do it–and with whom. If the "we" refers to the United Nations, it is salutary to be reminded of the remark of a Finnish minister of foreign affairs: "The word of the General Assembly, ECOSOC or their councils and commissions is a cry in the wilderness, unless the member states wish otherwise."

4. *Social pessimism* A mood which is dominant in radical Christian circles today considers global economic reform to be impossible in the context of a market economy. Social pessimists see markets as dehumanizing forces, constantly violating human dignity. According to F. Hinkelammert,

> the more the market violates human rights the more it has to expand so that the resultant violations of human rights continue to look like necessary steps on the road towards humanization through the market. Expanding the market also means accusing all the countries which do not submit to this market madness of constant violations of human rights, in order that these violations themselves can be understood as a condition for not succumbing to the despotism of those countries.[6]

In fact, the market can neither operate as a humanizing force nor violate human rights. Markets do not even produce output; they just set certain conditions for the coordination of supply with demand. The problem of the modern market economy does not lie in the mechanisms for free formation of prices as such nor even in self-interest. People can perceive their self-interest in the most inclusive manner. The real problem–already identified by Oxford 1937–is the enhancement of *acquisitiveness.* The crux of the matter is thus not to get rid of the market economy–for which we might have to wait a long time–but whether global capitalism can still be considered as *reformable.* Reform has to be inspired by vision; and after the collapse of real existing socialism there is an urgent need for new alternative visions.

The problem with these four moods is that they are all rather passive attitudes. None of them really inspires action. There is however another way of looking at our global predicament: the way of *global commitment* based on a global ethos, with structural reform resulting from processes of collective action. In this chapter we shall explore some visions that could inspire new strategies towards institutional reform in response to current global crises. In the final chapter we shall then examine some ways and means for relating Christian response to such civilizational perspectives.

Human rights and universal responsibility

Global norms upon which collective action for global care might be based were formulated in the Universal Declaration of Human Rights of 1948. In this declaration and in the international covenants which followed, economic, social and cultural rights are as important as the civil and political rights in which the international human rights project has its historical roots. Yet in practice the so-called second-generation rights tend to be ignored. One reason for this is that the judicial mechanisms created to implement civil and political rights are generally inappropriate for the realization of economic, social and cultural rights. Jurists usually see the latter as instructions to governments rather than as concrete entitlements on which to base subjective claims. Civil and political rights are regarded as a restraint on state power, whereas economic, social and cultural rights are considered to have a "promotional" nature requiring the state to take affirmative action. In fact, the implementation of civil and political rights also requires affirmative action on the part of the state – what is the meaning of press freedom, for example, if lack of resources means that marginalized people cannot get their opinions publicized? Similarly the state can also *violate* social, economic and cultural rights – through its food policies, for example.

Thus *waiting for the state* has become the never-ending story of second-generation human rights implementation. Although the norms are clear and unequivocal,[7] abundant excuses are at hand to explain why in certain situations these rights cannot be accorded to individual human beings. On the international plane, thinking about mechanisms for the realization of human rights norms has not progressed much beyond some reporting on socio-economic indicators. Waiting for the international community is thus taking a long time, as well.

In essence, the international human rights project is a global attempt to bind the execution of power to certain norms based on a universal belief in human dignity. Implementing these rights thus implies a continuous confrontation with power – and not only that of the state. Even more than first-generation human rights, second-generation rights are action-oriented. It is through processes of emancipation and collective action that such rights may be realized; and local struggles for the implementation of economic, social and cultural rights have in fact sometimes led to positive results. In a global context the challenge is essentially the same.

The human rights project bases such struggles on the notion of universal responsibility. In our global village, that responsibility is being taken up so poorly that the project itself has already lost a great deal of credibility. Acceptance of responsibility requires more than just a legal basis, no matter how universal. The ratification of treaties, the establishment of courts of human rights and the development of a human rights jurisprudence are not enough. The moral roots of the conviction which leads to responsible behaviour must be constantly nurtured by an ethos based on (not necessarily different) worldviews. To the extent that the notion of human rights finds its origin in individualism, it is "responsible" individualism that counts, which is evidently not the same thing as "possessive" individualism – the driving force of what R. H. Tawney called the "acquisitive society". Yet the former may easily degenerate into the latter.

Those cultures in which possessive individualism has strong roots – and this includes the "global village" itself – experience great difficulty with economic and social rights already at the stage of standard-setting. While individualism may offer sufficient moral foundation for respecting everyone's fundamental freedoms, it falls short as a basis for accepting other people's needs as a ground for justified claims. Economic, social and cultural rights presuppose not just free individuals but a community that accepts responsibility for the fulfilment of everyone's basic needs. In socially unstructured market economies, the weak find no structural protection against unemployment, disease, disability and old age. On what normative vision, then, may collective action for the implementation of economic and social rights be based? A first point of departure would seem to be social justice.

A widely known attempt to construct political principles of justice applicable to any society which tackles the problem of inequalities among people is that of John Rawls.[8] His "non-normative" theory is based on a hypothetical social contract between citizens who decide – behind a "veil of ignorance" regarding their relative success or failure in acquiring entitlement positions – what is socially "fair".

Without taking the space here to examine critically Rawls's rational-liberal theory of justice as such, we may note that it failed him when trying to construct a political "law of peoples" that would legitimate human rights on the basis of reason alone.[9] For one thing, he felt compelled to abandon the three egalitarian features of his theory of justice: the fair value of political liberties, fair equality of opportunity and the "difference principle", which stipulates that inequalities can be tolerated only if "they are to be to the greatest benefit of the least advantaged members of society". This limited his concept of human rights to civil rights, excluding political and socio-economic rights. He then argued that, if placed behind a veil of ignorance, even representatives of hierarchical societies, committed in a rather absolute sense to certain ideologies and religions, would accept the same "law of peoples", including basic civil rights, as democratic societies. But why would they? As Stanley Hoffmann puts the issue:

> Are societies whose governments are dogmatically committed to ideology or religion likely to respect basic human rights at all? Since there are no free elections, how would we know that their "system of law" meets "the essentials of legitimacy in the eyes of [their] own people"? Whatever the answer, what is clear is that

> Rawls's law of peoples has been shaped so as to appeal to a purely hypothetical group of peoples. The fallacy here is in the parallel Rawls seems to draw between an "overlapping consensus" of comprehensive doctrines that endorse a single conception of justice within a democratic political culture... and an "overlapping consensus" of *societies* based on very different political conceptions of justice. Such different societies could only endorse a very weak "law of peoples".[10]

For a stronger "law of peoples" it seems we cannot avoid looking for the conceptual foundations of human rights within the various religions in which notions of human dignity are rooted. Research done by Wronka would suggest that the idea of one person's responsibility for satisfaction of another person's needs is common to all world religions.[11] One example is the biblical notion of *tsedâqâ*, which implies acknowledgment of the claims of the poor purely on the ground of their need. But before exploring further whether religion may provide the necessary cultural basis for the human struggle for socio-economic rights, let us turn to a new social philosophical notion which may serve as the basis for the human rights struggle.

The decent society

Avishai Margalit makes a distinction between a civilized society and a decent one. A civilized society is one in which individuals do not humiliate each other; a decent society is one whose institutions do not humiliate its members. The notion of decency is thus related to the principle of eliminating humiliation. It presupposes that physical cruelty, resulting from a lack of respect for the human body, has already been eradicated. Humiliation is "any sort of behaviour or condition that constitutes a sound reason for a person to consider his or her self-respect injured". In Margalit's view the evils against which we have to guard

> centre on dehumanization–taking away people's control over their own lives, treating them like animals or machines and excluding them either from particular societies, or in the ultimate humiliation, from the human race as such.[12]

As a universal moral foundation for human rights, the decent society may well be more suitable than the concept of justice for consensus-oriented processes towards transformation of societies. It provides a criterion by which we can decide which institutional "injustices are morally intolerable".[13] Founded on respect for everyone, the decent society constitutes a paradigm that could assist in finding a new perspective for a world in disorder. In the area of economy, for example, it corresponds to the World Bank's definition of absolute poverty as "a condition of life so characterized by malnutrition, illiteracy and disease as to be beneath any reasonable definition of *human decency*".[14] Even seen in this minimal light decency is more than just an idea; it is an institutional programme based on universal responsibility. Hence it is relevant to the search for a global ethos as a moral basis of the international project for the implementation of human rights.

Before enquiring further into the implications of the decent society as a paradigm in a global context, we shall look at certain other relevant findings in our search for global perspectives of a civilizational nature.

Civil society

Michael Novak has also written about the issue of a decent human society.[15] Noting the ambiguity of the term "civil society", he distinguishes civil society today from that of the Habsburg era and the *ancien régime*, which was a euphemism for informal structures of power within a network of aristocrats. Novak prefers a civil society on the lines of the American model, with its "independent individual, the free and unconnected atomic self", a model he describes as "communitarian without being intensely communal". Its source lies in the capacity of all citizens to initiate cooperative activities with their fellow human beings – or, to put it in terms of Tocqueville's first law of democracy, the art of association as rooted in the social nature of the human being. Civil society is thus the primary agency of the common good, and the state is secondary. In this regard, the conception of churches as associations has gained considerable plausibility, Novak feels.

Noteworthy in this context is the relationship between democracy and religion, as argued by the French philosopher Pierre

Manent. When democracy emerged towards the end of the Enlightenment era, it demanded that religion be tolerated as long as it was individualized, privatized and relativized. Within two centuries democracy has been reduced to competition of interests and formalism in the sense of correct procedures. According to Novak, democracy shows no religious influence, since lacking a vision of a good society of free women and free men, it says little or nothing about the human being. Since religion has conformed to democracy's demands, democracy can make no complaints against it. The silence of democracy on the question of human destiny has therefore left the Jewish and Christian religions with a decisive advantage, for they do offer a view of the good society and a commitment to transcendent truth. From this truth people acquire their full identity, while just relations between them are guaranteed against their self-interests, which would set them in opposition to one another.

All the major contemporary themes are involved in Novak's approach: civilization, trust, freedom, responsibility, transcendent truth. He does not believe that a new mode of coexistence can be accomplished through technical or procedural means if it does not come out of more deeply held values, especially religious convictions. The question is, however, whether we are not facing a radically changed situation, to which classical liberal solutions do not give a satisfactory response.

Turning to the original spiritual sources

Our global civilization is fragile. Its interconnectedness consists not only in worldwide networks of communication but also in integrated modes of social, political and economic behaviour.

Francis Fukuyama, who became well-known for his declaration of "the end of history", now believes that human interaction, including the quality of social relationships, is the true driving force behind successful markets and democracies.[16] He develops this view in terms of "trust", "social capital" and "sociability" – the capacity of people to associate with each other and to shape not only their economic life but every other aspect of social existence. His treatise on trust represents growing attention to the need for economic life to be embedded in social life – a necessity Adam Smith had already elucidated more than two centuries ago (1776).

Vaclav Havel offers a more outspoken inspiration for renewal, elaborating a new model of global coexistence based on human transcendence. Havel views global civilization and global economic integration as no more than a thin veneer over the sum total of human awareness. The current civilizational achievements that may enrich us can equally impoverish, diminish and destroy our lives. Whether it is the splitting of the atom or the discovery of DNA, television or the computer, all discoveries can be turned against humanity and used to our detriment. This ambiguity generates the deepest uncertainties of our day.

Global civilization, according to Havel, must understand itself as multicultural, multipolar and at the same time truly global. This will be feasible only if humankind accepts a basic code of mutual coexistence, a kind of common minimum all can share. This must be an expression of the authentic collective will. It has to grow out of genuine spiritual roots hidden in our common global civilization. Havel is convinced that there is an essential similarity in the deepest roots of most if not all cultures, a genuinely unifying starting point for a new code of human coexistence, anchored in the great diversity of human traditions. This similarity can take shape if the will to do so manifests itself on a global scale. It consists of common elements such as respect for what transcends us – the mystery of Being or a moral order; certain imperatives that come to us from heaven, from nature, from our own hearts; respect for human dignity and for nature, a sense of solidarity and benevolence. In an address at Harvard University in 1995 Havel put it this way:

> We must come to understand the deep mutual connection or kinship between the various forms of our spirituality. We must recollect our original spiritual and moral substance, which grew out of the same essential experience of humanity.

In Havel's view this is the way to achieve an understanding among cultures that will enable them to work together in a truly ecumenical way to create a new order for the world. This he sees as the promising road towards a genuine renewal of our sense of responsibility for ourselves and for the world.

Havel thus reminds us of transcendence, of what we have suspected and projected into our forgotten myths and what perhaps has always been dormant within us as archetypes:

> That is, the awareness of our being anchored in the earth and the universe, the awareness that we are not here alone nor for ourselves alone, but that we are an integral part of higher, mysterious entities... This forgotten awareness is encoded in all religions. All cultures anticipate it in various forms. It is one of the things that form the basis of man's understanding of himself, of his place in the world and ultimately of the world as such.[17]

Here it is important to note the observation of Karl Rahner that transcendence also has its historicity.[18] The transcendental subjectivity of the human being is part of a changing reality. It cannot be understood unhistorically. In other words, there is no unchanging archetypal substance of transcendence. Without this sense of historicity (which does not manifest itself in Havel's reflections) transcendence easily becomes fixed in some unchangeable "forgotten awareness".

Freedom, goods and happiness

The meaning of transcendence in human life tends to be related to socio-political interpretations of freedom. Friedrich Hayek, the godfather of neo-liberalism, once wrote a book under the title *The Mirage of Social Justice*, in which he argued that only a negative notion of freedom – keep your hands off other people's property, allow everyone his or her liberty – can be more than a mirage. Is freedom then easy access to video and audio equipment, as Fukuyama once suggested? Is freedom earning a lot of money so that one has a wide choice of goods and can opt for many of them at the same time? Does freedom imply not making choices that cut off other options, indeed never committing oneself?

St Augustine believed that the principal good of a human being cannot be "bodily pleasure, nor absence of pain, nor strength, nor beauty, nor swiftness, nor whatever else is usually reckoned among the goods of the body".[19] The enjoyment of all these goods depends on something else: the soul. Indeed, happiness is the soul's enjoyment of itself, which comes into being as a relation with God:

"The perfection of all our good things and our perfect good is God." Hence happiness refers to a transcending reality. Ferguson expresses this in a similar manner: "Happiness... is a good which once obtained leaves nothing more to be desired." His central question is whether the inner reality traditionally defined as happiness exists any longer or has ceased to be part of human life in contemporary Western society. Indeed, happiness seems to be outmoded, superseded and difficult to translate. It cannot simply be identified with pleasure, satisfaction or fulfilment. In Ferguson's view, the idea that happiness is an invariable truth of the human condition has often been the ethnocentric arrogance of the Western mind.[20] His analysis of human history points to a series of different forms for the expression of social relations of transcendence, caught in terms of happiness.

> Every social relation is touched by transcendence, each exists in the face of the possibility of being other than it is. Any social relation, therefore, can find its own religious expression. But it is in the sphere of value that the most consistent religious forms are developed. This is not because value defines the good (as opposed to either the bad or the evil), and religion is in some sense an essentially moral discourse, but simply because value is the language of relative worth. It is, thus, a meta-language of relation, a category within which all other relations can be caught up and ordered.[21]

Seen from this angle, transcendence has to do with ultimate value. Thus a major concern is the emptying of value into mere things: the goods. People who live for goods fail to respect others as fellow human beings. This is illustrated by what Boff describes as the "pauperist concept" of the poor: identifying them with a lack of goods and not recognizing them as human beings with capabilities who are managing to survive in difficult situations. Another way of seeing the global poor is as *failures*, as people responsible for social disorder. A third way is to regard them as *victims* to whose welfare massive relief operations might be directed within the framework of modern charity. A fourth way of perceiving the poor is as a *threat*; thus De Swaan argues that the problems of ecological destruction and migration might convince the world's rich of the need for a global care system for the benefit of the poor.[22]

But it is doubtful that any of these ways of seeing other people will provide sufficient motivation for global collective action for social justice. There is, however, a fifth way of approaching them: as fellow human beings, that is, as people with the same *human* dignity and rights as we ourselves. Thus in a moral-political sense the principal question is not "What are these people lacking?" or "What problems will they cause?" or "What can we do for these poor devils?" or "What do we have to fear from individuals in such conditions?", but "How can their dignity and rights be realized?". Already during the age of the fathers of the early church Gregory of Nyssa spoke of the need to recognize the true identity of the poor:

> Do not despise them in their abjection: do not think them of no account. Reflect what they are and you will understand their dignity... The poor are the treasurers of the good things that we look for... They are the strongest of accusers, the best of defenders.[23]

This touches the core of the human rights project; and it is principally this project for the universal inclusion of people that might constitute the foundation for a new era of global commitment towards civilizational renewal.

Combined strategies: the public interest, justice and peace

Elias has argued that a "civilizing process" towards societies that function better in terms of our needs and purposes implies that social constraint becomes self-constraint and people (or states) perceive the common good (or, more appropriately, "the public interest") at a higher level.[24] The alternative is a fragmentation of the public interest into different parts, accompanied by a loss of self-restraint and increased polarization.

Indeed a revitalization of the public interest – defined by the Catholic bishops of England and Wales as the necessary societal context within which conflicting individual rights and interests can be weighed against one another or reconciled with each other – is urgently needed today. According to the bishops, "the common good is contradicted if any section of the population is excluded from participation in the life of the community even at the minimum level".[25] Such a wrong must be remedied.

The public interest, then, is public justice *incognito*. In our contemporary world public justice means realizing justice in global society. In the next chapter we will look more closely at both public interest and public justice in terms of the global social and economic situation. Here we refer to the norm of *peace*. Unlike the Greek word for peace (*eirene*), which alluded to the period of relative calm and tranquillity between wars, the Hebrew *shalom* and the Arab *salaam* have a much deeper meaning, in which peace is perceived as being founded on right relations between individual human beings as well as peoples, while also connected with well-being and welfare.[26] Where order and justice are disturbed, there can be no peace. Peace implies freedom from fear. Its opposite is not simply war or violent conflict, but discord, disaster and misery.

In such a perspective the challenge is to find combined strategies to combat the global crises of deepening poverty, environmental destruction and social disintegration. This will involve not primarily representatives of states around their conference tables but all sections of the global population. All types of actors – individual citizens, corporations and non-governmental organizations as well as states – will have to be part of such a process of civilizational reorientation. The question now is what role religion in general and Christianity in particular might have to play here.

NOTES

1 F. Fukuyama, "The End of History?", *The National Interest*, Summer 1989, pp.3-18.

2 F. Fukuyama, *The End of History and the Last Man*, New York, The Free Press, 1992.

3 S. Sato, "Clash of Civilizations", *loc. cit.*, pp.1-2.

4 An example is Paul Kennedy's disappointing book *Preparing for the Twenty-First Century*, London, Harper-Collins, 1993.

5 Typical of this social optimism are Mahhub ul Haq's remarks about the Bretton Woods institutions: "*We must* form alliances for change within these institutions... *We must* convince these institutions to focus more on human development strategies"; "New Imperatives of Human Security", unpublished paper for the Stockholm Roundtable of the UN De-

velopment Programme (22-24 July 1994) in preparation for the 1995 world summit for social development (italics added).

[6] In *Sacrifice and Humane Economic Life*, an Occasional Study Paper of the WCC's Commission of the Churches on Participation in Development, 1991.

[7] Cf. "The Limburg Principles on the Implementation of the International Covenant on Economic, Social and Cultural Rights", *Human Rights Quarterly*, Vol. 9, no.2, May 1987.

[8] John Rawls, *A Theory of Justice*, Cambridge, Mass., Harvard U. P., 1971.

[9] Cf. S. Shute and S. Hurley, eds, *On Human Rights: The Oxford Amnesty Lectures 1993*, New York, Basic Books, 1995.

[10] Stanley Hoffmann, "Dreams of a Just World", *The New York Review of Books*, 2 Nov. 1995, p.54.

[11] Cf. J. Wronka, *Human Rights and Social Policy in the 21st Century*, Lanham, Md., University Press of America, 1992.

[12] As summarized by A. Ryan in a review of Margalit's *The Decent Society* (tr. Naomi Goldblum, Cambridge, Mass., Harvard U. P., 1996), in *The New York Review of Books*, 11 July 1996, p.19.

[13] M. Ignatiew, "The Necessary Sting: Problems of Erasing Humiliation in a Decent Society", *Times Literary Supplement*, March 1997, p.10.

[14] World Bank, *World Development Report 1980*, p.32, italics added.

[15] Cf. M. Novak, "The Future of Civil Society", *Crisis*, Oct. 1996.

[16] F. Fukuyama, *Trust: The Social Virtues and the Creation of Prosperity*, New York, The Free Press, 1995.

[17] "The Need for Transcendence in the Post-Modern World" (address at Independence Hall, Philadelphia, on US Independence Day), 4 July 1994.

[18] Karl Rahner, *Foundations of Christian Faith: An Introduction to the Idea of Christianity*, tr. W. van Dyck, London, 1978, p.140.

[19] Cited by H. Ferguson, *Religious Transformation in Western Society: The End of Happiness*, London and New York, Routledge, 1992, p.x.

[20] *Ibid.*, p.1.

[21] *Ibid.*, p.205.

[22] A. de Swaan, *In Care of the State: Health Care, Education and Welfare in Europe and in the United States in the Modern Era*, Oxford, Oxford U. P., 1990.

[23] Cited by W. Walsh and J. P. Langan, "Patristic Social Consciousness", *loc. cit.*, p.130.

[24] Cf. N. Elias, *State Formation and Civilization*, Oxford, Basil Blackwell, 1982.

[25] Catholic Bishops Conference of England and Wales, *The Common Good and the Catholic Church's Social Teaching*, 1996.

[26] B. V. A. Röling speaks of "positive peace" as opposed to "negative peace" in the sense of the absence of war, in "Armament, Disarmament, Development and Security", in B. Goudzwaard, ed., *Economics, Armament and Development*, Alphen a/d Rijn, NL, Samson, 1985.

7. The Globalization of Religion and Civilizational Change

Social teaching is not limited to a collection of official, mainly papal, texts. It is an oral tradition as well as a written one, and it is a lived and living tradition. Those whose lives are dedicated to the service and welfare of others make this teaching present by their very activity, even if they have never read a social encyclical.

Catholic Bishops Conference of England and Wales (1996)
The Common Good and the Catholic Church's Social Teaching, para. 28

From world religions to global religions

Global technological, political and economic developments have brought types of progress that have contributed much to the lives of many people. We may think here of the impressive discoveries of modern science, of successful struggles against tyranny, of the establishment of democratic institutions and of human development in the sense of widening the options in many people's lives. But on the other hand, there is also

> the blind worship of perpetual economic growth and consumption, regardless of their destructive impact on the environment, or how subject they are to the dictates of materialism and consumerism, or how they, through the omnipresence of television and advertising, promote uniformity and banality instead of respect for human uniqueness.[1]

Awareness is growing that consumerism has become a dominant global ethos in the sense of setting the moral style and mood of global society.[2] Any ethos and the daily patterns of action connected with it are embedded in a "symbolic universe": a cosmology which establishes "a connection between the reality of everyday life and a higher, usually supernatural world which is taken to be the foundation of everything".[3] In the case of modern mass consumerism–*the ethos of the goods*–individualistic materialism may be seen as the sustaining cosmology, in the sense that it has grown from an attitude into a world view. Leonardo Boff calls it developmentalism, which "views human beings as mere producers and consumers of material goods. It has no heart, no compassion, no sense of solidarity, no sensitivity to catch the message coming from the universe."[4]

Here we touch the fundamental juxtaposition between the goods and God which constitutes the focus of this study. Boff speaks of the need to base ourselves on a broader view of what constitutes humankind.

> Either we relate to one another, understand the universe as a web of very complex relationships, nature as a tissue of subtle connections where everything has to do with everything else at all times and in all situations, and human society as being built upon multi-directional networks of relationships, or else we shall experience the fate of the dinosaurs, who disappeared because they were incapable of relating to a changed situation. Out of this capacity and the need to establish relationships, there will be a renewed understanding of religion (religion is all about relationships) as that human institution that is a repository of the experience through the ages that everything is related to the Supreme Reality, thus creating a sense of life and the universe as one global reality.[5]

Rather than thinking of just an animal species – the dinosaur – humankind today may be reminded of the fate of the Hohokam Indians, who lived in what is now central Arizona until the 15th century. Their name means, in the Pima language, "those who have gone". Indeed, it seems quite likely that their whole civilization perished because they destroyed their own environment. Apparently they built cities (including four-storey buildings), traded with their neighbours and managed an impressive system of agriculture in the desert on the basis of irrigation. The white settlers who arrived in Arizona around 1800 still found the ruins of their canals, but the Hohokam had disappeared. It is taken that they either ran out of water or, while using and recycling it, destroyed the ecological balance between water and soil.[6]

Some of the key concepts in Boff's new design of liberation theology are the globalization of a cosmic experience of time and space, the perception of interrelationships and a basic attitude of surprise in reaction to mystery. "Mystery" refers to the Spirit in its original significance, expressing the totality of the human being in terms of energy, meaning and vitality. Spirit, in other words, is not set over against body but over against death. Spirituality, then, means living in oneness with the inner dynamics of life, in the totality of relations to others and to all life within the cosmos. These "life dynamics" also become manifest in dialogue with the deeper self, and with the mystery inside us that we term God. This spirituality, with all these diverse dimensions in a dynamic process, constitutes the integrity of the person as well as the integration with everything around.[7]

At this point we may recall Margalit's notion of "the decent society". As he sees it, this concept does not demand any spiritual or moral justification, since the requirement of eradicating all cruelty, including humiliation, constitutes the paradigm example of moral behaviour.[8] Unfortunately, reality contradicts the view that the decent society could embody a global ethos without any further need to be sustained and nurtured by a spiritually oriented worldview. Even cruelty and institutionalized humiliation have become part of the structural patterns of everyday life. In terms of human practice no global ethos of decency significantly manifests itself. Hence, as a moral minimum for judging the quality of politics, even the decent society needs supporting links with belief systems such as Boff's cosmocentric view.

For Boff social and political liberation are vitally important but not sufficient for the complete liberation of both the human being and society. Integral liberation must include a uniting perception and experience of total reality. Boff has developed a remarkable view of this process: it is *ecological thinking* that should enable us to construct an integrating idea and to understand that everything which exists actually *co*-exists within the most encompassing system of the cosmos. In this interconnectedness and in the globalization of this consciousness lies the alternative to Western forms of modern rationality.[9]

Boff thereby both broadens and radicalizes spirituality. The inner connection of the human being with God is not nurtured by the Bible alone, or by meeting God in the poor and excluded, or through the history of the suffering and liberation of peoples. This inner bond also has its roots in the movements of the cosmos which feed the deeper self of the human being. Boff thus shifts the emphasis in the spirituality of liberation theology from an anthropocentric foundation to a cosmocentric focus. Spirituality nurtures another way of viewing the subjectivity of human beings and their inner selves. Indeed, the core experience of the Spirit takes shape in the forces working in the inner vitality of human beings and their social and cosmic connections.

Thus from Vaclav Havel and Leonardo Boff to John Paul II the view is expressed that the spiritual dimensions of human life can and should lead to a better, more authentically human society, once the Spirit works in all peoples – believers as well as non-believers – and connects them to the universe. The overriding concern is evidently the urgent need for a new spirituality within a global culture in crisis. Since politics follows culture, the primary task is not the political struggle within the global framework but rather transformation at the cultural and spiritual levels. Indeed, in Havel's and Boff's views, it is transcendence that might provide a genuine foundation for a cohesive global humanity and for a global politics that can justifiably be expected to meet the needs of different societies.

Before looking at three types of current religious responses to globalization, we should make a few preliminary remarks on the globalization of religion. In the first place, as we have seen, globalization is both continuous with and discontinuous from modernization. Hence global religion cannot escape the *modern* nature of our world. Jürgen Moltmann has identified three ways in which modernity challenges religion: the unprejudiced application of modern science in the search for truth, the principle of individual responsibility as opposed to religious coercion and the rejection of hierarchies that suppress individual freedoms.[10]

Second, a global religion must confirm its relationship to the whole world in a focus on all people wherever they live. In other words, it has to be a religion of West and East, North and South.

Third, global religion, says Moltmann, has to be a *religion of the earth*. It is in response to ecological crises and threats that people today are searching for a global environmental focus in religion. Boff speaks in this connection of a new state of awareness that provides a foundation for building up a relationship of goodwill, solidarity and love with the earth.[11]

The challenge, then, for each of the major world religions is to become truly *global*. Obviously, this is incompatible with pretensions to and claims of exclusive uniqueness. If Christianity is to have an impact on global civilization, it must accept its position as *one* of the major social and religious forces that shape people's world views. A truly global focus would foster an end to both Eurocentrism and anthropocentrism. No longer could uniform doctrines simply be imposed on the majority of Christians living in Africa, Asia and South America. The Orthodox Church will have to abandon its claim to possess the only "true doctrine", the Roman Catholic Church its claim to be the only "true Church", and the Protestant churches their claim to preach the only "true faith".[12]

Three types of religious response to globalization

Globalization has provoked a variety of religious responses, which attempt to revitalize and adapt religious notions for changing contexts. One of these is *fundamentalism*, which signifies an increase in politicized religion, especially when religion is invoked as a basis for identification with territories and associated cultures. *Syncretism*, by contrast, signifies a tendency towards de-territorializing religion, eliminating the identification of religious groups with territories and associated cultures. A third response, *ecumenism*, is indicative of a relativization of particular religions in the sense of a relative loss of significance of each religion separately. Its background lies in the prevailing impossibility of ignoring the part played by other universal religions at the global level.

Fundamentalism. We must begin by acknowledging that the label "religious fundamentalism" is not an entirely satisfactory one, and may even be misleading when it is used to group together many phenomena[13] and overlap different versions of a religion. Religious militancy and conservatism, for instance, may refer to the same phenomenon. "Fundamentalism" is an Anglo-Saxon term, generally applied to those who believe that their holy book – for Christians the Bible, for Muslims the Quran – must be interpreted literally. Often in fact "religious fundamentalism" amounts to "little more than a label of convenience" used to describe and explain resistance against materialism and secularism.[14] But for lack of a better term we cannot escape from it.

The question is whether or not – and if so to what degree – people are engaged in a "search for fundamentals". Is there a growing universal concern with "ultimate values"? And is this an aspect of globalization? Does the search for fundamentals slide inevitably into "fundamentalism"? Or, on the contrary, if we recognize that people currently *are* in search of fundamentals, do we not thereby put those people – ourselves – in a very safe place, far away from "fundamentalism"?[15]

Our chief interest in this study is the global nature of the current search for fundamentals. "Fundamentals", according to Roland Robertson, have to do with tradition, identity, home, indigeneity, locality, community, "going native", finding one's place in the world as a whole.[16] Finding a place, defining one's right to identity, involves attempts to attain *power*. The search for identity may well be a claim to power, at least to empowerment. Hence it may involve the display of all kinds of resources. But when does the search for fundamentals take the form of an exclusive search for original traditions?

Globalization contributes both directly and indirectly to the worldwide development of fundamentalism. The type of fundamentalism that emerged in the former decades transmits the *discontents* of modernization and post-modernization to religious traditions.[17] These discontents include economic failure, political authoritarianism and the failure of the state to provide for basic needs, improve social welfare and offer prospects for the future.

But fundamentalism also resists the displacement of older values that are no longer appropriate by the establishment of new values. Some scholars consider fundamentalism as inherently reactionary, using traditional faith as its vehicle, venerating the wisdom of the past, reasserting old truths and former certainties, dreaming of the recovery of a mythical golden age in order to set things right.[18] But it is inadequate simply to describe all fundamentalist religious groups as reactionary. Most of them do seek social and political change, express the undesirability of modern Western transformations (such as gender equality) and link the change that is called for to the words of the holy books.

The resurgence of religious fundamentalism, in sum, can be differently interpreted: as a *reaction* to globalization and/or an *aspect* of it. In the former sense, fundamentalism may be seen as a way to express identity and resist globalization. When we treat fundamentalism as an aspect or consequence of globalization, we consider it as being built into the general process of globalization.

Syncretism. As a response to globalization, syncretism re-integrates elements from diverse religious traditions, often associating these with current life-styles in a fluidity of organizational forms. However, one must be very cautious about using the label syncretism for practices or rituals one does not understand.[19] One of the great contemporary challenges is precisely to develop non-coercive, non-manipulative ways of studying other cultures.[20]

Syncretism basically refers to a fusion of diverse religious beliefs and practices. The original use of the phrase was in the realm of politics. The Greek philosopher and moralist Plutarch (46-120 C. E.) used it for the assembling of the normally divided people of Crete in order to face a common external enemy. Today, it is typically employed to designate the intermingling of two or more traditions or worldviews.[21] Syncretism is not limited to the mixing of religions; it can also be used in relation to the mixing of cultural traditions and ideologies.

An historical illustration of syncretism comes from Aztec culture at the time of the Spanish conquest. The most elaborated aspect of Aztec culture was its religious system. Much of Aztec religious ideology drew on earlier and contemporary cultures of Central America; and Aztec civilization was in a continuous process of assimilating and reorganizing its religious traditions, demonstrating a remarkable measure of reformability. One of the most famous symbols of this came to be the Virgin of Guadalupe (Mexico). The Yoruba religion in Western Africa, voodoo in Haiti and Umbanda in Brazil are also considered to be syncretistic religions. Candomblé and voodoo have been considered the most specific forms of African syncretism in the Americas, as different groups, subjected to forced migration, invoked not only their own gods but also practised rites other than their own, creating new religions through the integration of their beliefs.

While the term "syncretism" is not found in the Bible, examples of religious syncretism are evident in both the Old and New Testaments. Just as the early gods of the Vedas represented natural forces, so the Canaanite deities known as Baal and the God of the Hebrews were first seen as storm gods. God came to be recognized not as a Lord of nature but as a Lord of history. The capacity to judge history required a transcendent deity.[22] Through much of their history the people of Israel accepted elements from both these traditions, producing their own highly syncretistic religion.[23] From the time of the prophet Amos onwards, the religion of Israel was marked by a tension between the concept of monotheism and the universal ideal of salvation for all nations on the one hand, and the notion of God's special covenant with the people of Israel on the other. As a movement within Judaism, Christianity began during a period when the Jews had long been under foreign rule and influence. An intensified syncretism can be seen in the New Testament: the multi-religious context of the early church confronted it with many religious imports into its faith. Warnings against teachers, doctrines and practices with syncretistic tendencies abound throughout the letters of Paul and others.

Contemporary discussions of syncretism, especially in ecumenical circles, have been highly controversial. Some have noted that the expressions of virtually all religions are permeated with syncretistic elements. The problem with interpreting the term so broadly is that syncretism then becomes an umbrella phrase which loses any analytical value or descriptive potential. If virtually every expression of religion is syncretistic, it becomes meaningless to say so. There is also a positive interpretation of syncretism – which some would dismiss as romantic – as a harmonious integration of all faiths, a solution to sectarianism, nationalism, ethnocentrism and religious intolerance.[24]

Within the Christian churches, debates about syncretism often turn around the attempt to distinguish it from *inculturation*. For example, in her presentation at the seventh assembly of the World Council of Churches (Canberra 1991) the Korean theologian Chung Hyun-Kyung invoked the spirits of those who had suffered and died, the "spirit of earth, air and water, raped, tortured and exploited by human greed for money" and ended her call to "listen to the cries of creation and the cries of the Spirit within it" with the words: "Come. The spirit of the Liberator, our brother Jesus, tortured and killed on the cross." She concluded her address with a description of her own "image of the Holy Spirit", coming from the image of Kwan In, venerated as the goddess of compassion and wisdom by women's popular religiosity in East Asia. Representatives of Orthodox churches and many others objected to her presentation as syncretistic and insisted that syncretism in all its manifestations and circumstances must be repudiated as a misleading distortion of the Christian faith. While inculturation of the gospel is seen as desirable and necessary, it is evident that a definitive borderline between inculturation and syncretism cannot be drawn.[25]

Ecumenism. The term "ecumenism" points to a quest for worldwide unity or cooperation. In the early centuries "ecumenical" was used to refer to the universality of the Christian churches; in the 20th century it has been applied to the movement which has worked for the visible unity of the divided Christian churches, which gave birth to the World Council of Churches in 1948 and to many similar organizations and initiatives at the local, national, regional and global levels. The word comes from the Greek *oikos*, meaning "house", "family", "people". In the context of religion it usually implies a renewal of faith traditions, a removal of ignorance and prejudice and an encouragement to religions to rethink their attitudes towards one another.

The ecumenical response to globalization affirms religion as part of contemporary resources for combatting world poverty, exclusion, environmental destruction and civil strife. In this perspective interfaith collaborative efforts seek to increase dialogue and cooperation between the competing convictions of different faith communities and worldviews.

There are several reasons to regard this era as an opportune time for deepening ecumenism.[26] In the first place, religious extremism is now seen as an important item on the political agenda rather than a concern for religious professionals alone. Second, the collapse of communism seems to have made the United Nations open to religious influence in an unprecedented way; and many people working in UN agencies now agree that there are spiritual and moral dimensions to the great problems facing our world. Third, the interfaith movement has a new outward-looking concern. Fourth, a growing number of religious leaders are publicly acknowledging the importance of inter-religious understanding and cooperation.

The Parliament of World Religions, convened in Chicago in 1993 to mark the centenary of a similar initiative there in 1893, recalled the emergence of various proposals over the past decades to establish a world religious body. The basic idea is a simple one: to work together to overcome centuries of misunderstanding, division and violence and to support each other's efforts for peace. However, no real breakthrough has yet emerged from such existing world bodies of faith as the World Congress of Faiths, the Temple of Understanding, the World Conference on Religion and Peace, and the World Council of Faiths. The difficulty of finding a co-operative structure for interfaith organization lies in the need for a mandate from the whole range of interfaith organizations and the authority to address international policy issues. This would require the initiative, commitment and dedication of the leaders of several religions and not just their representatives. It would also need the active support and involvement of international political and economic leaders.

There are indeed several reasons to doubt that the creation of a world religious body would in fact effectively enhance religious response to global crises. How could such an organization avoid being bureaucratic and "Western" rather than multi-centred? Which communities are to be recognized as "religious"? This was already a problem at the Chicago parliament, where the presence of certain new religious movements induced some Orthodox representatives to pull out. Who would constitute the leadership of a world council of faiths? Some religions have clearly designated leaders (like the pope and cardinals of the Roman Catholic Church) while others (Hinduism, for instance) are not structured in such manner. Another concern is that religious influence is often weakened by religious disagreement; for example, it is far easier to agree on the need to end poverty than on the methods of birth control that may be necessary to achieve this. Thus more understanding is needed of the religious, philosophical, historical and cultural backgrounds that shape the approaches of different faith communities as well as adequate expertise on the issues discussed.

Nevertheless, the various religious initiatives for interfaith coordination – whether or not they are focused on the creation of a world body – manifest a growing awareness that the world's religions must contribute to meeting the multiple crises facing the world today. Although religious leaders may not be in a position to propose detailed solutions, they might yet assist in creating an international conscience that demands effective political action.

Within the global system religion can be *anti-systemic* and *pro-systemic* at the same time; that is, it can foster globalization by opposing its effects. This requires reorientation of the religious traditions: openness to change is seen as contributing to the continued authenticity of the tradition. In opposing the marginalization of their religion in the context of globalization, people assert their particular identity as a religious group or collectivity, which is as such a principal method of competing for power and influence in the global system.[27] By taking up the values of an emerging global culture, religion re-articulates itself.

We are now ready to turn to the major focus of this study: the possible contributions which Christianity might make to the needed global civilizational change. The basic elements of the conflict of values between Christianity and global capitalism should have become sufficiently clear. The question therefore arises: is Christianity, or more specifically its body of social ethics and teaching, indeed a motivating force in the search for a new social and global cohesion and a new ecological awareness? Or has the public and political dimension of Christianity become insignificant and irrelevant in the contemporary global context? On this both the US bishops and the bishops of England and Wales offer some remarkable perspectives.

Basic justice for all

In *Economic Justice for All* the US Catholic bishops stipulate as a requirement of basic justice that people be assured of a minimum level of participation in the economy (para. 15). The pastoral letter distinguishes three dimensions of basic justice with converging demands: commutative justice, distributive justice and social justice (para. 68).

- *Commutative justice* calls for fairness in all sorts of agreements and exchanges between individuals or private social groups and demands respect for the equal human dignity of all persons in economic transactions, contracts and promises (para. 69). This means that workers owe employers their work in exchange for wages and that employers must offer their employees conditions of work that are truly human while paying them fair wages.
- *Distributive justice* requires that the apportionment of income, wealth and power in society be evaluated according to its effects on unmet basic needs (para. 70). This grows out of the teaching of the early church that the community has an obligation to help fulfil basic needs unless an absolute scarcity of resources makes this strictly impossible. We are *obliged* to come to the relief of the poor, and not merely out of positions of affluence.
- *Social justice*, sometimes called "contributive justice", stresses the responsibility of all to help create the goods, services and values necessary for the welfare of the whole community. Not only do men and women have an obligation to be active and productive participants in the life of society, but their work should also enable them to develop their humanity fully. Therefore, society has a duty to enable all to participate, which requires that social and economic institutions be ordered in a way that guarantees this (paras 71-72, 78). Productivity is thus measured not only by its input in resources and output in goods and services but also by its impact on the fulfilment of basic needs, employment levels, patterns of discrimination, environmental quality and sense of community.

From these interconnected forms of justice the US bishops conclude that justice in society is tested by its treatment of the poor:

> The obligation to provide justice for all means that the poor have the single most urgent economic claim... Personal decisions, policies of private and public bodies, and power relationships must be all evaluated by their effects on those who lack the minimum necessities of nutrition, housing, education and health care (paras 86, 90).

All of us must therefore examine our own way of living in the light of the needs of the poor. In other words, Christian faith and the norms of justice impose limits – on what we consume, on how we view material goods and on how we treat others.

Basic justice, then, involves the task of overcoming patterns of exclusion and powerlessness so as to guarantee participation of all in society. This means that we have to commit ourselves to the common good (or the public interest) and to replace a common ethic of individual rights with an *ethic of the common good.*

An ethic of the common good

The common good (*bonum commune*) has regained a significant place in debates on future social and economic perspectives, illustrating a growing sense that a lack of commitment to the common good is at the roots of the contemporary socio-economic crisis. The notion originated in the writings of Plato, Aristotle and Cicero. The Christian social tradition has a long history of specifying, advancing and encouraging the common good – from the writings of the fathers of the early church to papal encyclicals to documents of the World Council of Churches. John Rawls has recently reinterpreted the idea by connecting it to the ideology of political liberalism. In a broader sense, orientation towards the common good is at the heart of most discussions of business ethics, environmental pollution, health and education systems.

The common good consists of practices, systems and institutions which have a powerful impact on the well-being of society and on which all depend: accessible health care, just legal and political procedures, prosperous economic systems, an unpolluted natural environment and clean air, public security and peace. The common good is a collective and global good to which all members of all societies should have access and from whose enjoyment no one can be excluded. Already in the 1960s the Second Vatican Council defined the common good within a new context of interdependence:

> Every day human interdependence grows more tightly drawn and spreads by degrees over the whole world. As a result *the common good, that is, the sum of those conditions of social life which allow social groups and their individual members relatively thorough and ready access to their own fulfilment*, today takes on an increasingly universal complexion and consequently involves rights and duties with respect to the whole human race. Every social group must take account of the needs and legitimate aspirations of other groups, and even of the general welfare of the entire human family (*Gaudium et Spes*, para. 26, italics added).

The bishops of England and Wales reconfirm and elaborate this definition in their 1996 document on *The Common Good and the Catholic Church's Social Teaching:*

> That common good is the whole network of social conditions which enable human individuals and groups to flourish and live a fully, genuinely human life, otherwise described as "integral human development". All are responsible for all, collectively, at the level of society or nation, not only as individuals... The concept of an international or global common good demands that no nation should be left incapable of participation in the global economy because it is too poor or too much in debt (paras 48, 102).

Advancing the common good calls for prudence and care. As Pope John XXIII pointed out in Pacem in Terris (1963), individual citizens, intermediate groups and state authorities must bring their own interests into harmony with the needs of the community:

> Indeed, since the whole reason for the existence of civil authorities is the realization of the common good, it is clearly necessary that, in pursuing this objective, they should respect its essential elements, and at the same time conform their laws to the circumstances of the day (paras 53, 54).

Pacem in Terris cites the statement of Pope Leo XIII that "the civil power must not serve the advantage of any one individual, or of some few persons, inasmuch as it was established for the common good of all", but then goes on to suggest a corrective to this along the lines of what today would be called affirmative action:

> Considerations of justice and equity, however, can at times demand that those involved in civil government give more attention to the less fortunate members of the community, since they are less able to defend their rights and to assert their legitimate claims (para. 56).[28]

Market forces and the common good. In regard to economic market forces, Catholic social teaching has always remained cautious. Left to themselves, market forces can create bad or good results. They can be an efficient mechanism for prosperity and for linking resources to needs but they must always be evaluated and corrected in the name of basic justice and the common good. In any case, since markets do not operate in a value-free society, the English and Welsh bishops insist that any belief in their automatic benefits is to be rejected (para. 77). An adequate functioning of the market rather requires ethical principles and behaviour within a regulatory and legal framework. Thus, the common good

> provides criteria by which public authorities can distinguish between those economic activities that can safely be left to market forces, and those that require regulation, state intervention, or full provision by the public sector... It is always the business of public authority to arbitrate between the sometimes conflicting demands of a market economy and the common good (para. 81).

According to the English and Welsh bishops, the public authorities have the common good as their prime responsibility (para. 70). In concrete terms this demands fair international trading policies, decent treatment of refugees, support for the United Nations, control of the arms trade and equality of rights and opportunities (para. 14).

The global common good. Establishing the common good in the sense of maintaining social conditions from which all benefit requires cooperative efforts of citizens. "Common" implies "all-inclusive"; that is, no one may be exempted from the duty to support the common good nor excluded from the right to benefit from it (para. 70).[29] But the bishops also insist that in addition to the duty of every member of the community towards the common good in order that the rights of others be satisfied and their freedoms respected, there is also a responsibility to help those whose rights and freedoms are being denied to claim what they need (para. 37). All have the right to participate in the formation of public policies.

The concept of a "global common good" requires that no nation be left incapable of participating in the global economy (para. 102). Too much reliance on free market principles in economic relations between *unequal* international partners causes injustice. International cooperation and regulation are needed in processes of transition to full participation in the global economy. According to the bishops of England and Wales this includes refraining from imposing economic adjustment programmes on the poorest countries, opening Western markets to products of the South, supporting appropriate regional security structures and ensuring care for the environment (paras 105-106). In this global context the bishops also identify the dumping of human "social capital" within the framework of "downsizing" operations of companies as a widespread cause of global social injustice.

Obstacles. Several major factors which hinder society and its members from maintaining the common good may be noted here. The first is the so-called *free-rider* problem. Free-riders are those people who take the benefits of the common good but refuse to assume their own share of providing it. This happens, for example, in the field of social security and welfare. If the number of free-riders in a society is high, the common good will be destroyed.

A second obstacle, linked to the first one, is the *unequal sharing of burdens*. The common good may demand that the cost borne by specific groups greatly exceeds that of others. For example, creating equal employment opportunities may require that white males sacrifice part of their own employment chances or accept lower salaries. The probability of having to carry such burdens may induce strong resistance to efforts to establish or protect the common good.

A third underlying obstacle is that the common good is sometimes seen as incompatible with *pluralism* in society. Efforts to evoke a sustained and widespread commitment to the common good encounter not just differences of emphasis but serious disagreements about what constitutes the collective good and thus about what kinds of systems and institutions are needed to promote it. In the realm of public policy, some would prefer to invest more in health care, others in education, still others in environmental protection. Is it possible to avoid excluding some while endorsing the views of others?

But while these obstacles are serious challenges to the establishment of a well-functioning system of democracy, they cannot serve as an excuse to escape from responsibilities towards the realization of the common good.

Civilizational perspective: the problem of Christian commitment

We have seen that the social teaching of the Christian churches offers abundant resources to inspire, orient and encourage the transformation of global capitalism: the priority it gives to the human over the economic, its continuous resistance to economic determinism, its concepts of justice and the common good. Underlying the contributions of the social teaching of the churches is the re-establishment of the economic world within the framework of social ethics and its subordination to the common good (cf. *Mater et Magistra*, para. 37). The common good is incompatible with a belief in the automatic benefits of free-market capitalism. Furthermore, the human person cannot be reduced to a commodity or to a mere producer or consumer conforming to market requirements. The rights to decent work, just wages, limitation of hours of work, health and safety protection, not to mention the right of non-discrimination, are all prior to the rights of capital.

We have also seen that the teaching authority of the churches, however pertinent it may be, is limited in its practical socio-economic application; and we have suggested that this is in part due to an underlying discrepancy between the social teaching of the Catholic Church and its approach to sexual ethics.

Global solutions based on global ethics. Vaclav Havel has pointed to a growing awareness that what humankind needs most today is a common sense of spirituality and duty. According to Havel, a new spirit (understood in a secular anthropological sense) is emerging: a spirit which connects people instead of dividing them, inspiring them towards coexistence and human interaction. Out of this spirituality he sees a basic code of global human coexistence emerging, a kind of common minimum all can share. Others, like Hans Küng and the 1993 Parliament of World Religions, have spoken of a similar search for a kind of basic global ethic based on cooperation between world religions.[30] Still other efforts have recently culminated in the submission of a proposed Universal Declaration of Human Responsibilities to the secretary general of the United Nations by the Interaction Council.[31] All these proposals converge in the conviction that global solutions to global problems require the establishment of an ethical base and the formulation of a set of moral standards. Among the many questions that face such global initiatives, one is very pertinent: will a global ethos which emphasizes prescriptive rules in fact promote the coexistence of global humanity?

The idea of developing a Declaration for a Global Ethic was launched by the Council of the Parliament of the World's Religions in Chicago in 1993, which brought together leading representatives of the historic religions of the world. The Council plans to hold periodic "parliaments of religion" in different parts of the world (the next will be in South Africa in 1999) and continues to promote the "Declaration Towards a Global Ethic" prepared by Hans Küng and signed by most of the 200 delegates in Chicago. Earlier in 1993, at an annual meeting of a Jewish-Christian-Muslim dialogue in Graz, Austria, a similar document had been presented by Leonard Swidler, entitled "Universal Declaration of a Global Ethic". To make their documents as representative as possible of a global consensus, both Küng and Swidler consulted representatives from the world's major religious traditions.[32] Both hoped that other declarations would be formulated in the future, and thus considered their own documents only as the beginning of a process.

In a certain sense, the Chicago conference saw the Declaration Towards a Global Ethic as *complementary* to the Universal Declaration of Human Rights. Some would go further to suggest that a new United Nations Declaration on a Global Ethic be issued to provide moral support for the Universal Declaration of Human Rights.

Riffat Hassan has made some critical observations about the conceptualization and methodology of this Declaration Towards a Global Ethic, and its supposed complementarity to United Nations declarations on global issues. Whereas the new declaration would be grounded in religion, the Universal Declaration of Human Rights does not acknowledge religion as a source of human rights and indeed evidently sought to distance itself from any sort of identification with religions, which had contributed to so much division and strife in the world.[33] Hassan agrees with the World Conference for Religion and Peace in criticizing the failure of the United Nations until recently to see that human rights become meaningful only when placed within the framework of people's worldviews.[34] A major reason why the Universal Declaration of Human Rights is so thoroughly ignored in everyday human behaviour, she argues, is that it has not been grounded in the lives of so many peoples in the world. Although she recognizes the existence of the Universal Declaration of Human Rights as an outstanding achievement of humanity as a whole and sees a declaration towards a global ethic as a similar achievement, Hassan also asserts that such declarations alone cannot bring about moral or social transformation. From her Muslim perspective, any kind of ethics begins at home, with oneself, with the specificity and complexity of the lives and beliefs of others, particularly those who are seen as adversaries or aliens.

A second criticism Hassan levels against such declarations is that they are not the products of a dialogue with each religion about its central ethical concerns and principles, but emerge from contemporary Western Christian perspectives. Hence, they do not reflect the ethos of the religions of the world. Along the lines of John Hick's plea for other independent drafts from the cultures of China, Africa, Russia, India, the Islamic world, the Buddhist world and the primal life streams, Hassan underscores the challenge of finding ways to open the discussion with all the great traditions of the earth on an equal basis.

An ethos of public service. The main position we would take here is not a global ethos (in the sense of a set of norms and standards formulated by a few and imposed from above) but an ethos of public service as a major public asset, which must be promoted by a combination of different strategies. In global society the common good and public service must be lifted to an international level. What recent efforts towards global ethics seem to overlook is the loss of confidence in the public arena, in local communities and intermediate institutions, and the retreat from the public level to the private sphere.[35] This tendency implies a weakening of a spirit of partnership and teamwork, cooperation and interaction. To resist this, the bishops of England and Wales present a provocative proposal: "the political arena has to be reclaimed in the name of the common good" (*The Common Good*, para. 119). It is indeed the *quality* of politics that is at stake, both globally and in regional, national and local contexts.

The test of every practice and policy, system and institution is whether it enhances or threatens human dignity and the common good. Public authorities are primarily accountable for the common good which they have to guard and promote. All must accept their full share of responsibility to provide for the common good of society, enabling others to realize their dignity and achieve their rights. The first responsibility of citizens towards the common good and towards public justice is therefore not to promote a global ethics but to ensure that no one is marginalized or excluded. It is the failure to recognize this duty which results in an "urban underclass", a *massa sobrante* living in destitute conditions, in contrast to the social and economic privileges of the others.

Towards a new commitment. But how can people be enabled to resist the global trend and to identify and counter collectively the structures of injustice, discrimination and inequality in their own societies?[36] How is the lack of belief in core values and principles of a good society to be overcome? Utopian socialists have often too quickly offered generalized theories and practices of "collective action" and "empowerment" as the foundation for sustainable public policy. The communitarian movement and the Christian Democratic parties in Europe have tried to avoid the question by pointing to a responsible society, civic responsibility, or the primacy of obligations over rights. Liberal idealists seek to transform society by a sort of social engineering: the ability of government and organizational programmes to orchestrate a good society through broad social agendas. But neither civic responsibility (communitarianism), social engineering (liberal idealism) nor collective action (utopian socialism) seems to promise an adequate instrument for global change.

Citizens have discovered new approaches to managing resources, protecting the environment, providing health care, regulating markets, conducting political affairs. Such initiatives are based on ethical principles of redistribution and interconnectedness. New networks of citizens will possibly crosscut existing power structures. Thus, a more promising way forward than the three approaches mentioned above is to take seriously the obstacles to realizing the common good cited earlier–free-riding, unequal sharing of burdens and pluralism–and to advance an approach of citizens' self-commitment, intrinsically linked to a similar commitment by *others*, in the context of the public interest. This involves combined policies and strategies towards socio-economic transformation which account more fully for the connection between the dignity of each individual person, the particular interests of the group, the collective concerns of society and an involvement with global environment.

With economic power centralized at the global level while political power continues to be linked to national and local levels, economic and political power have to be brought into balance in very distinct contexts. From the angle of public justice and the common good, this is not a simple option in between centralizing global power and decentralized local or national power. Rather, it implies what Aristotle called *oikonomia*: the management of a household, aimed at extending its contribution to the collective needs over the long run. This means that abundance and prosperity are limited by the needs of others. The balancing of power thus requires that the notions of public interest, global sustainability and care for future generations are deeply rooted in recognition of basic needs and public justice, as components of the common good.

In the light of religious, cultural and social differences it does not seem likely that citizens will find consensus at the global level on one common ethical orientation. Can we in this context fully appreciate the need to integrate religion in efforts towards public commitment? While opinions are divided about a religious basis for social cohesion and fair social cooperation between citizens, there seems to be less disagreement about the need for transcendence – overcoming anthropocentrism – and genuine spirituality in establishing a foundation for the universal common good.

Mission in foreign structures

During discussions of the churches' response to the global crisis at the WCC's seventh assembly (Canberra 1991), when some delegates were advocating the creation of new institutions, Patrick D'Souza, Catholic bishop of Benares, pressed for caution. "We Christians are fully part of the structures of our time," he remarked. "The challenge now is to change these structures from within. While Christians used to send missions to foreign countries, the test today lies in mission into *foreign structures*, in the sense of institutions and institutional arrangements that must be considered *foreign* to the gospel of justice and love."

Naturally, this type of "missionary" activity would have to be pursued in a manner quite distinct from the classical model of Christians who have already seen the light going out to all those others who are still blind – in this case to the structural injustices in which their lives have been caught. What is at stake here is the intended third stage of the "conciliar process for justice, peace and integrity of creation" set in motion by the WCC's sixth assembly (Vancouver 1983) – the stage of concerted efforts to seek cooperation with all other forces for structural renewal directed at justice, peace and integrity of creation: trade unions, non-governmental organizations for societal change, political parties committed to reform, movements for economic democracy and so forth. It was there, however, that the process got stuck. One reason for the failure to broaden that "conciliar process" may well be that the churches did not give the impression of being open to "inner mission" – in the sense of having something to learn from the many others engaged in struggles for an effective response to a world in disorder.

Mission to "foreign structures" will have to mean more than a series of unconnected commitments by scattered individuals. The churches will be required to support initiatives for change of a civilizational nature through the activities of already existing bodies such as the Pontifical Commission for Justice and Peace, Pax Christi and the World Council of Churches, in close cooperation with regional and national councils of churches and of course other local churches. It is evident that the time is not ripe for Catholic-WCC collaboration in a single movement (such as took place in the joint committee for Solidarity, Development and Peace, SODEPAX, in the 1970s). It is an open question whether full institutional cooperation at the highest levels is even desirable. But we should be aware that in the search for new civilizational perspectives the old lines of division among Christians do not seem particularly relevant; and new initiatives must be taken in *ecumenical* types of cooperation at whatever place or level. It is high time, moreover, to implement the objective of broadening Christian efforts towards justice, peace and integrity of creation.

A theological approach to Christian cooperation with Muslims, Jews, Hindus, Buddhists, humanists and others may be developed from the notion of the "civil or political use of the law of the Lord".[37] Through Moses the law was given to the people of Israel, but, as St Paul implies time and again, it was also inscribed in the hearts of the whole human race (cf. Rom. 2:25-29). A true believer is a person whose whole practical orientation in life shows that his or her heart is attached to the law. It is evident that while its own members often constitute hindrances on the road towards peace, justice and the integrity of creation, those outside the Christian church frequently appear to follow law and gospel in their lives. Trees are known by the fruits which they produce. It is from this perspective that we now wish to conclude our study with some biblical observations on *God and the goods*.[38]

Rich towards God

The transformation of societies is not a simple process, as the post-communist events in Eastern Europe have amply demonstrated. Transformation of the globe is still another matter. The adjective "human" is being used increasingly to indicate the scope and nature of the issues at stake: *human* development, *human* security, adjustment with a *human* face. Indeed, the challenge remains a matter of *humanization*, which implies the realization of basic human rights while assigning each person his or her proper responsibilities, neither too much nor too little.[39]

Clearly, there is no panacea which will cure all global ills simultaneously, and any new ideology or policy that claims to offer an immediate and all-embracing impact on the direction of global developments should be distrusted. Nevertheless, we have come across certain insights that could contribute to the search for transformation in a global civilizational perspective. Major prospects appear to be offered by different types of local response to a commitment to the global common good. The churches may learn from and join forces with other institutions and people working towards public justice at the planetary level.

However, the central question which we posed at the outset is still largely unanswered: what specific role might be expected from Christianity and its principal institutions, the churches? In response, let us come back to the theme which serves as the title of the book: *God and the goods*.

The source of our title is the parable recorded in Luke 12:13-21. Jesus told this story after someone made a request that reflected an obsession with material gain. The rich fool of the tale says to his own soul: "You have ample goods laid up for many years; relax, eat, drink and be merry" (Luke 12:19). Then God calls him: "Fool! This night your soul is required of you; and the goods you have prepared, whose will they be?" (v.20). Verse 21 then reveals the crux of the matter: a juxtaposition between the goods and God. The real distinction is between storing up treasures for ourselves and being rich towards God.

Of course the point of this story is not that it would in any way be better to be without goods. Christianity does not support a type of "slave morality" which considers the humiliation of poverty to be a formative experience fostering humble attitudes to life.[40] What is problematic is not the goods as such but the fact that they are available only to the one who gathered them for himself. This is greed, of the sort to which the letter of James refers in a vivid warning:

> Come now, rich people, weep and wail for the miseries that are coming to you. Your riches have rotted, and your clothes are moth-eaten. Your gold and silver have rusted, and their rust will be evidence against you, and it will eat your flesh like fire. You have laid up treasure for the last days. Listen! The wages of the labourers who mowed your fields, which you kept back by fraud, cry out, and the cries of the harvesters have reached the ears of the Lord of hosts. You have lived on the earth in luxury and in pleasure; you have fattened your hearts in a day of slaughter. You have condemned and murdered the righteous one, who does not resist you (5:1-6).

This text speaks of collecting goods through exploitation, driven by pure acquisitive greed. Addictive possession of goods undermines compassion and social justice. Christian social teaching emphasizes the need for a change from an obsession with material goods to a detachment from them. We are the stewards, not the owners, of what we possess. To be rich towards God implies accepting an inclusive community in which the goods are available for common use. Indeed, the right to material goods or property can never be an absolute right; we are using what belongs to us and others in common, we are using what belongs to the poor and excluded. Our material goods have to serve the needs of all. This is what John Chrysostom referred to when he declared: "Write this message in our minds, on our walls, on our hands, in our consciences – write it everywhere."[41]

As Denys Munby showed in *God and the Rich Society*, the roots of our global predicament lie not in poverty as a separate "problem", but in undue and unjust ways and means of getting and being rich. This applies both to individuals[42] and to institutions and countries ("Fortress Europe", for example). As we saw in an earlier chapter, wealth today tends to be mobile, secret and hidden, elusive and inaccessible, completely insulated from the needs and claims of the poor. Here another parable of Jesus is appropriate – that of the rich man and Lazarus (Luke 16:19-31). It records the story of a wealthy man in whose life a poor person appears at the margin every day. After death their roles appear to be reversed:

now it is Lazarus who enjoys a good life while the rich man suffers. The point is not that poor people will be better off in the world to come, but that the rich can save their souls only by listening to "Moses and the prophets" here and now. Today there are hundreds of millions of poor people at the doors of the rich. But even their most minimal claims, based on utter destitution, are not accepted. The presence of the rich in the lives of the poor is of a purely negative significance. They refuse to follow the law of God; and hence they lose their souls.

"To be rich towards God" implies a renewed acknowledgment of God. Reference may be made here to the biblical notion of *da'at elohim.* This is not an abstract knowledge which one might acquire through study. *Da'at elohim* stands in a line with *'emet* (truth in the sense of faithfulness) and *hesed* (love in the sense of intense loyalty to the others). *Da'at elohim* signifies a basic relationship to God, a continuous *walking with God*, as Enoch did in all his activities (Gen. 5:22), a desire to recognize God and to walk on the paths of righteousness. People who walk with God do not necessarily engage in other types of activities, but what they do, they do walking with God, which means walking with the poor.

The mentality of acquisitive greed has taken root in the structures of global capitalism. The challenge now is to work towards an incorporation of a different mentality–based on social justice, compassion and generosity (*caritas*)–in the structures of contemporary society. This is the issue on which the churches should concentrate their concern with economic matters today: the use and abuse of wealth and resources on the one hand, and processes of exclusion, impoverishment, environmental destruction and social disintegration on the other.

One concern here is how religious thinking and acting are themselves affected by the goods one possesses. "I fear wherever riches have increased, the essence of religion has decreased," wrote John Wesley. And St Paul admonishes: "Religion may make people very rich, provided they are satisfied with what they have. What did we bring into the world? Nothing! What can we take out of the world? Nothing!" (1 Tim. 6:6-7).

In making decisions today about material affairs, who takes the hundreds of millions of poor and excluded people into account, who thinks of duties towards the earth, who cares about future generations? Vaclav Havel formulates the question pointedly:

> Who worries about what people will eat, drink, breathe a hundred years from now, or where the energy will come from as the world population doubles? We are told that only idealists and dreamers have such concerns, and that they are people out of touch with the modern world. Those dreamers, who are often at the margin of society though their books may be widely read, will find their way to where they belong, among the politicians, only if the very spirit of politics changes and moves towards a deeper sense of responsibility for the world.[43]

Do the churches share these concerns? Could they contribute to a change of the very spirit of both politics and economics? Living within the "foreign structures" of our time Christians could perhaps contribute to a new understanding of the true purpose of our existence on this earth and of our deeds as the spiritual foundation for developing new models of behaviour, new scales of value and life objectives.

The famous expression of Thomas Hobbes that "man is a wolf to man" (*homo homini lupus*) refers back to an adage – from centuries before Christ – of Caecilius Statius: "Man is a god to man when he recognizes his duty" (*homo homini deus est si suum officium sciat*). To be rich towards God means recognizing claims founded on fundamental freedoms and basic needs. Above all it means recognition of *duty*. From "living for the goods" to living in response to needs and hence in recognition of duty: there we meet the principal challenge of a global civilization at the crossroads. Is there any possibility of meeting that challenge? While humans are asked to turn to God ("Turn to God – Rejoice in Hope" is the theme of the WCC's eighth assembly in 1998), Christian hope lies in the God who has turned to human beings. While humans continue to seek the goods, God appears to continue looking for good human beings and to call them to their duty. It is in this central message that Christianity may find inspiration today to contribute to new civilizational perspectives.

NOTES

[1] Vaclav Havel, "The Charms of NATO", *The New York Review of Books*, 15 Jan. 1998, p.24.
[2] Cf. C. Geertz, *The Interpretation of Cultures*, New York, Basic Books, 1973.
[3] A. de Ruijter and L. van Vucht Tijssen, "Culture and Development: An Ambivalent Alliance", in de Ruijter and van Vucht Tijssen, eds, *Cultural Dynamics in Development Processes*, The Hague, Nuffic/ Netherlands National Commission for UNESCO, 1995, p.6.
[4] L. Boff, "A New Alliance Between Humankind and Nature", *Echoes* (WCC), 1997, pp.23.
[5] *Ibid.*, p.27.
[6] For the story of the Hohokam Indians, see Marc Reisner, *Cadillac Desert*, London, Penguin Books, 1993.
[7] Cf. L. Boff, *Ecologia, Mundialização, Espiritualidade: A Emergência de um Novo Paradigma*, São Paulo, Ed. Atica, 1993, p.139; J. van Nieuwenhove, "Bevrijding en de crisis van paradigma's: Mondialisering ter discussie", *Tijdschrift voor Theologie*, Vol. 38, no. 1, 1998.
[8] Margalit, *op. cit.*, p.88.
[9] Cf. L. Boff, *Ecologia, Grito da Terra, Grito dos Pobres*, São Paulo, Ed. Atica, 1995; "Theologie der Befreiung und Ökologie: Alternative, Gegensatz oder Ergänzung?", in R. Fornet-Betancourt, ed., *Befreiungstheologie*, Vol. 2, *Kritische Auswertung und neue Herausforderungen*, Mainz, Matthias Grünewald, 1997, pp.339-49.
[10] J. Moltmann, "Christianity in the Third Millennium", *Theology Today*, Apr. 1994, pp.75-89.
[11] "A New Alliance", *loc. cit.*, p.23.
[12] Moltmann, *loc. cit.*
[13] J. Haynes, *Religion in Third World Politics*, Buckingham and Philadelphia, Open University Press, 1993, p.33.
[14] *Ibid.*, p.36.
[15] R. Robertson, *Globalization*, pp.164ff.
[16] *Ibid.*, pp.166-67.
[17] Haynes, *op. cit.*, pp.35f.; cf. Waters, 1995, p.130.
[18] Haynes, *op. cit.*, p.36.
[19] A. Scott Moreau, "Syncretism", ms. for entry in *Evangelical Dictionary of Theology*, rev. ed. (forthcoming), 1998, p.4.
[20] G. Viswanathan, "Beyond Orientalism: Syncretism and the Politics of Knowledge", in *SEHR*, Vol. 5, no.1, 1996, p.1.

[21] Scott Moreau, *loc. cit.*, p.2.

[22] See K. Armstrong, *A History of God from Abraham to the Present: The 4000-Year Quest for God*, London, Heinemann, 1993.

[23] For example, Psalm 82 depicts God as sitting in the assembly of gods (*elohim*): "God has taken his place in the divine council; in the midst of the gods he holds judgment" (v.1, NRSV). This psalm is usually interpreted as illustrating the transition from polytheism to monotheism; cf. Th. Booij, *Psalmen: Prediking van het Oude Testament*, vol. 3, Nijkerk, NL, Callenbach, 1994, pp.16ff.

[24] Viswanathan, *loc. cit.*, pp.1f.

[25] For the text of her address and a summary of reactions see M. Kinnamon, ed., *Signs of the Spirit*, official report of the WCC's seventh assembly, Geneva, WCC, 1991, pp.37-47, 15f.

[26] The following paragraphs draw on Marcus Braybrooke, "A World Body for the World Religions? A Historical Perspective", unpublished paper for an international interfaith conference in Oxford, Apr. 1996.

[27] Cf. Beyer, *Religion and Globalization*, pp.3f.

[28] A justification for this is already found in *Mater et Magistra* (1961), where John XXIII wrote that the state, whose *raison d'être* is "the realization of the common good in the temporal order... cannot hold aloof from economic matters" and has the duty "to protect the rights of all its people, and particularly of its weaker members, the workers, women and children" (para. 20).

[29] On the relationship between justice and the common good see also *Divini Redemptoris* (1937), where Pius XI wrote: "It is of the very essence of social justice to demand from each individual all that is necessary for the common good" (para. 51).

[30] See B.Klein Goldewijk, ed., *Religion and Conflict: Religion in the Generation, Growth and Resolution of Conflict*, Kampen, NL, Kok, 1998; and H. Küng, *Global Responsibility: In Search of a New World Ethic*, London, SCM, 1991.

[31] The Interaction Council met in Vienna in April 1997 and was chaired by former German chancellor Helmut Schmidt. For the text of its draft declaration, see *Current Dialogue* (WCC), no.31, Dec. 1997, pp.47-55.

[32] Cf. R. Hassan, "A Muslim's Reflection on a New Global Ethics and Cultural Diversity", in *The Power of Culture: "Our Creative Diversity"*, Amsterdam, KIT Report, 1996, p.4.

[33] An attempt by the Dutch delegate de Beaufort, a Roman Catholic priest, to amend the preamble with a reference to "man's divine origin and his eternal destiny" was rejected – and would, indeed, have been out of place in the Universal Declaration, which stems from a secular tradition

originating in the thought of the European Enlightenment. Its starting point is the fundamental freedoms of the individual, which must be protected against the power of the sovereign (the state). Although the final articles of the text do refer to the community and the individual's duties in regard to it, the gist of the Declaration remains individual-centred.

34 Cf. B. de Gaay Fortman, "Human Rights and Religion", in B. Klein Goldewijk, ed., *Religion and Conflict.*

35 Cf. B. Klein Goldewijk and B. Schennink, "Liberation from Exclusion: Prospects for Civil Society", in *Liberation from Exclusion: Proceedings of a Conference on Liberation from Below in Latin America and Eastern Europe*, Nijmegen, NL, Peace Research Centre, 1993, pp.213-27.

36 Cf. B. Klein Goldewijk, "Consolidación o crisis de las estructuras eclesiales de base? Nuevas estructuras eclesiales sin reconocimiento oficial", in *Concilium*, no. 243, 1992, pp.839-48.

37 Cf. G. Rothuizen, *Primus Usus Legis: Over het Burgerlijk Gebruik der Wet*, Kampen, NL, Kok, 1962. According to this understanding, the civil and political use of the law is the "first" – the *primus usus legis*; the second is that through the law we recognize that we are sinners in need of God's mercy; the third is that Christians express their gratitude for the mercy God has shown by attempting to follow the law in their personal lives.

38 This theological approach may provide a less pretentious grounding for socio-cultural, political and socio-economic cooperation between Christians and others than the way in which the Catholic Church declares certain people of good will to be its "implicit" members – which follows from the claim to be the only true Church in combination with a misinterpretation of the doctrine that outside the church there is no salvation. Since Vatican II this fiction of *vota implicita* may be regarded as outdated; cf. A. Houtepen, *God een open vraag*, Zoetermeer, NL, Meinema, 1997, p.383.

39 Cf. Denys Munby, *God and the Rich Society*, London, Oxford U.P., 1961, p.177.

40 Although this idea may seem to be behind Christian practice, for example, the way Christian Dalits in India have sometimes been told by church hierarchies to accept their lot in life is totally contrary to biblical thinking. Cf. Margalit, *op. cit.*, pp.26f.

41 Cited in Walsh and Langan, "Patristic Social Consciousness", *loc. cit.*, p.131.

42 The number of billionaires in the world increased from 57 to 447 between 1989 and 1996; and according to the 1996 UN *Human Develop-*

ment Report, the total wealth of the world's ten richest persons is one-and-a-half times the national income of all the Least Developed Countries together.

43 V. Havel, "The Charms of NATO", *loc. cit.*